The Leaseholders H

CONTENTS

Introduction

1 The lease. What it is and how it works   11

2 Respective obligations of leaseholder/freeholder   19

3 Service charges and the law   33

INTRODUCTION

Over the last 30 years, the law covering leasehold property has developed in a manner which has given more and more protection to leaseholders. This protection was seen as necessary because all too often leaseholders have been victims of poor management by (often) unscrupulous landlords, particularly in the area of service charge delivery and management of service charge accounts.

In the public sector, there has been a marked lack of knowledge and resultant management problems, particularly in the area of service charges, and only now has it been seen as necessary to promote this area as a specialism.

Since the 1960's, laws have been introduced designed to provide a regulatory framework for the dealings between freeholder and leaseholder, initially concerning the acquisition of the freehold of properties, by leaseholders, and in the 1980's in the area of the provision of service charges and overall management. The 1985 Landlord and Tenant Act, as amended by the 1987 Landlord and Tenant Act, provides for a series of steps which landlords must observe when spending service charge money of leaseholders in their blocks

It is surprising how many freeholders and leaseholders live in ignorance of their rights and obligations, even though such a significant body of legislation exists to protect those rights.

In 1993, the Leasehold Reform and Urban Development Act extended those rights initially granted in the 1967 Leasehold Reform Act to the purchase of the freehold and extension of leases. Collectively, leaseholders can purchase the freehold of a block (enfranchisement) and individually leaseholders can extend their leases by a given number of years past its existing life.

These steps are clear but can be problematic and are described in full in this book.

In May 2002, the Government introduced the Commonhold and Leasehold Reform Act, which introduced new legislation protecting leaseholders amending the 1993 Leasehold Reform Act. This Act introduces the 'no fault' right to manage where, subject to certain criteria leaseholders can take over the running of their flats, without having to prove fault. A new form of ownership is also introduced, 'commonhold'. The Act is discussed in detail in Appendix 2.

The general principles covering the setting up of a flat management company, and how to run a company effectively, are also outlined. This is a natural follow on to the acquisition of the freehold of a block, whether by enfranchisement or voluntary sale.

Overall, the book is designed to raise the awareness of leaseholders who wish to understand what is often a complex relationship between landlord and tenant, and also to help landlords understand their own obligations.

1

THE LEASE AND HOW IT WORKS

Chapter 1

The Lease-What it is and How it Works

Freehold, Commonhold and Leasehold

The strongest form of title to land is that of freeholder. Freehold title lasts forever; it may be bought and sold, or passed on by inheritance.

Freeholders can use their land for other purposes. They may also, if they wish, allow other people to use their land, usually through a lease or tenancy.

A lease grants the leaseholder permission to use the land for a certain period, which can be anything from a day to several thousand years. It will usually attach conditions, for example, that the leaseholder must pay rent (usually a sum of money). The lease may, but does not have to, put certain restrictions on what the leaseholder may do with the land. But it must, in order to be a lease rather than merely a licence, grant the leaseholder 'exclusive possession'. This is the right to exclude other people, especially the landlord, from the land. Such a right need not be absolute, and exceptions to it are explained later in the book: but it is enough to give the leaseholder a high degree of control over the land, which has become, for the duration of the lease, very much the leaseholder's land rather than the freeholder's.

A lease, unless it contains a stipulation to the contrary, may be bought, sold, or inherited; if this happens, all the rights and duties under it pass to the new owner.

A new form of ownership, that of commonhold, was

introduced by the Commonhold and Leasehold Reform Act 2002. Commonhold means that the purchaser of a flat in a block will own the flat in which they live, much the same as the leaseholder but will have no lease as such. They own their property in perpetuity along with common ownership and an obligation with other commonholders, to maintain the common parts. Although this book is concerned mainly with the rights of the leaseholder, most of the issues will concern the commonholder, as they deal with the maintenance of common parts.

Leases and Tenancies

Confusion is often caused by the fact that, although the terms leaseholder (or lessee) and tenant are legally interchangeable, they tend to be used in different senses. The tendency is to refer to short leases as tenancies: the more substantial the rights conferred, and the longer the period for which they run, the more likely it is that the agreement will be referred to as a lease.

It is common for private landlords to insist on prepayment of rent or a deposit before granting a tenancy, and almost all landlords will levy a service charge to cover the cost of some activities that are peripheral to the central one of providing housing; but despite these costs it would be true to say that the principal financial responsibility accepted by a periodic or short-term tenant is that of paying the rent.

The position of a leaseholder is very different. The major financial commitment will usually be a substantial initial payment either to the landlord (if the lease is newly created) or to the previous leaseholder. This is normally done through a mortgage. There is still a rent, called a ground rent, payable to the landlord, but it is usually a notional amount (£50 a year is not uncommon). Its purpose is not so much to give the landlord an income as to give the leaseholder an annual reminder that ultimate ownership of the land is not his.

The leaseholder is only liable, under the provisions of the 2002 Commonhold and Leasehold Reform Act, to pay ground rent on receipt of a demand from the landlord.

Different types of Leasehold Property

The great majority of leases relate to flats rather than houses. Where flats are sold, each purchaser acquires a lease that gives him specified rights over the parcel of land on which the flats stand. These rights, of course, are shared by the leaseholders of the other flats. In addition, however, each leaseholder gains the right to exclusive possession of part of the building occupying the land - his own flat.

The freehold of flatted property will often be retained by the developer, although sometimes it will be sold to a property company. Formerly, it was common practice for the freehold to be retained even when separate houses were built. This allowed the freeholder to retain an interest in the property and, above all, to regain full possession of it when the lease expired. However, the position of freeholders has been weakened by two several key pieces of legislation, the Leasehold Reform Act 1967 the Leasehold Reform, Housing and Urban Development Act 1993, and the Commonhold and Leasehold Reform Act 2002. These Acts are described in detail in Chapter Four: their overall effect is to entitle leaseholders either to the freehold of houses or to a new lease of flats. In view of the legislation, there is now little point in the original owner attempting to retain the freehold of land on which houses have been built. The exception is where a house is sold on the basis of shared ownership - see below.

Most residential leasehold property therefore consists of flats. Of these, most are in the private sector, comprising purpose-built blocks and (especially in London) conversions of what were once large single houses. The freehold will usually belong to the developer, to a property company, or sometimes to the original owner of the site.

House leases normally give most of the repairing responsibility to the leaseholder - services provided by the freeholder, and therefore service charges, are minimal. In flats, however, although the leaseholder will normally be responsible for the interior of the flat, the freeholder will maintain the fabric of the building and will recoup the costs of doing so by levying service charges on the leaseholders. This is an area of such potential conflict between leaseholders and freeholders that it has been the subject of legislation, which is discussed further on in the book.

The right to buy

The general shift from renting to owning meant that sometimes flats have been sold in blocks that were originally developed for letting to tenants: the result is often a 'mixed-tenure' block, with both leaseholders and tenants. Although this sometimes happens in the private sector, it is particularly common in blocks owned by local authorities and housing associations, for it is to these that the statutory right to buy applies. This right was created by the Housing Act 1980 and allows local authority tenants, and some housing association tenants, to buy their homes at a heavily discounted price. Tenants of houses are normally sold the freehold, but tenants of flats become leaseholders. More recently, a similar but less generous scheme has been introduced covering many housing association tenants not already qualifying for the full right to buy. Purchasing a council home has been, for most of the million or so that have done so, a very satisfactory investment. A minority of purchasers have, however, met with serious difficulties, particularly where they have become leaseholders in mixed tenure blocks of flats. Chapter Three looks at some of the problems affecting management and service charges.

At the time of writing, the government is once again trying to kick-start right to buy, by offering large discounts of up to £75,000. The idea is that for every public sector property sold two are built to replace it, although serious doubts have been raised about the feasibility of this.

Shared ownership

Another result of the trend towards home ownership was the dramatic expansion of shared ownership. This has tailed off and currently, purchasers of shared ownership property have the same problems as purchasers of other property, lack of mortgage opportunities.

Shared ownership is a form of tenure that combines leasing and renting. However, the term 'shared ownership' is something of a misnomer because ownership is not, in fact, shared between the leaseholder and the freeholder. The lease relates to the whole property, not part of it, and the shared owner is as entitled as any other leaseholder to consider himself the owner of his house. The key point about shared ownership leases is not that they give an inferior form of tenure to other leases but that they have different conditions attached. The leaseholder pays less than the full value of the lease; typically, half. In exchange for this concession, he pays not the normal notional ground rent but a much more substantial rent. However, he is much more a leaseholder than he is a tenant, and, like other leaseholders (but unlike tenants) is responsible for the internal repair of the property and, in the case of houses, usually the fabric of the building too. Shared owners usually have the right to increase their stake as and when they can afford it: this is called 'staircasing' because the owner's share goes up in steps. If the property is a house, the freehold will normally be transferred when the owner's share reaches 100%, and he will then be in the same position as any other freehold homeowner. If it is a flat, he will continue to be a leaseholder but there will no longer be a rental (other than ground rent).

Head Leases and Subleases

It is the right of the leaseholder, unless the lease specifically forbids it, to sublet the property, or part of it, to someone else. This means that the leaseholder has delegated some of his rights over the property to another person. Obviously, he cannot delegate rights greater than his own, and he cannot grant a sublease of the whole of his rights because this would leave him with no interest in the property: it would, in fact, amount to the same as an assignment. So it is necessary for a sublease that the original leaseholder be left with something; either some period of time or some part of the property.

2

RESPECTIVE OBLIGATIONS OF THE LEASEHOLDER AND FREEHOLDER

Chapter 2

Respective Obligations of Freeholder and Leaseholder

For centuries the law did little to regulate the relationship between freeholders and leaseholders. The view was taken that they had entered into the relationship of their own free will, and it was up to them to agree whatever terms and conditions they liked.

In the twentieth century, however, the view has grown up that some types of bargain are inherently unfair and even those that are not may still be open to exploitation.

An example of the first type is an agreement that residential property will revert to the original freeholder at the end of a long lease. This meant that when 99-year leases expired, leaseholders found that their homes had abruptly returned to the outright ownership of the heir of the original freeholder, leaving them as mere trespassers liable to be ejected at any time. In practice, freeholders were usually willing to grant a fresh lease, but sometimes only at a very high price that the leaseholder might well be unable to afford. In some cases, freeholders insisted on reclaiming the property however much the leaseholder offered, and the law supported them. This is the state of affairs that led to legislation entitling almost all residential leaseholders to extend their leases, and many of them to claim the freehold. This is dealt with in Chapter Four.

The freeholder's right to demand a service charge is an example of an arrangement that is fair in principle but open to abuse in practice. It is inevitable, especially in flats, that responsibility for some types of repair cannot be ascribed to any individual leaseholder and must therefore be retained by the freeholder; who must, in turn, recoup the cost from leaseholders. However, some freeholders abused this system by levying extravagant service charges that made the service charge as a source of profit. To prevent this, there is now a substantial body of legislation designed to ensure that freeholders carry out only the works that are really necessary and that they recover their legitimate costs and no more. The complicated rules governing this are chiefly found in the *Landlord and Tenant Act 1985 (as amended) the Housing Act 1996 and the 2002 Commonhold and Leasehold Reform Act. These are described in Chapter Three.*

Under the Landlord and Tenant Act 1987, either party to a long lease (one originally granted for at least 21 years) may go to court (or Leasehold Valuation Tribunal) to argue that the lease is deficient in some way and needs to be changed. If only the one lease is affected, the court may vary it. Sometimes, however, a number of leases may need to be changed; in this case either the freeholder or 75% of the leaseholders may apply.

Where the law is silent, however, it remains the case that the lease can contain any covenants or conditions that the freeholder can induce the leaseholder to accept.

Obligations of Leaseholders

Leases have been drawn up at different times and vary depending on prevailing legal practice and on the chief concerns of the freeholder at the time. However, similar terms are found in typical leases

a: Onerous conditions

This is a term applied to conditions that have the effect of seriously reducing the value of the lease. Such a condition is not necessarily an unreasonable one; it may serve some legitimate purpose. But no one should sign a lease containing them without fully understanding their likely effect.

A common example of an onerous term is a restriction on the kind of person to whom the lease may be sold (or 'assigned' - see below). For example, a housing scheme may have been intended specifically for the elderly. Clearly, it could not be maintained as such if leaseholders were free to assign or bequeath their leases to whomever they please, so the lease will say that it may be assigned only to persons above a certain age, and that if it is inherited by anyone outside the age group it must be sold on to someone qualified to hold it. Although this could be described as an onerous term because it makes it more difficult to find a buyer and may reduce the lease's value, it is reasonable given the need to ensure that the scheme continues to house elderly people exclusively. And the restriction it imposes is not too severe because so many potential purchasers qualify.

However, some leases define much more narrowly to whom they may be sold. Sometimes the freeholder is a body owned and run by the leaseholders themselves, and in these cases it is usual to require that all leaseholders must join the organisation and, if they leave it, must immediately dispose of the lease to someone that is willing to join. Again, such a term is not necessarily unacceptable. If the organisation makes relatively light demands on its members (perhaps no more than a modest admission fee or annual subscription), the restriction is unlikely greatly to diminish the value of the lease. If, however, the organisation expects much more from its members - perhaps that they actively take part in running it, or that they pay a large annual subscription - the value of the lease will be severely reduced because it will be difficult to find purchasers willing to accept the conditions. A key point is whether the organisation has power to expel members, thus forcing them to sell; and, if so, in what circumstances and by whom this power can be exercised.

b: Blanket conditions

Slightly different from the onerous condition is the blanket condition. It is common for leases to contain sweeping provisions that would, if they were enforced, give the freeholder considerable control over the leaseholder's life. For example:

- *Pets* Leases often lay down that the leaseholder may not own pets, or may not do so without the freeholder's permission.
- *Business Leases* often lay down that the leaseholder must not run any sort of business from his home.
- *Use as residence.* A lease will generally say that the property is to be used for residential purposes, and will sometimes attempt to restrict how many people may live there apart from the leaseholder.

It is easy to see why freeholders want such clauses in the lease. But the kind of blanket rules that appear in many leases go too far. A rule against any pets at all forbids not only noisy dogs but also inoffensive pets such as a budgie or a goldfish. In the same way, prohibiting business activities means that the leaseholder may not use his home to write a book for publication, or address envelopes, and so on - types of home working that could not possibly inconvenience anyone. The reality is that this kind of provision is seldom enforced. Freeholders, and their lawyers, like it because they feel that it preserves their freedom of action, allowing them to decide whether or not to enforce the lease if it is clear that one of these blanket conditions is being broken.

c: Access

Virtually any lease will contain a clause allowing the freeholder to enter the property in order to inspect or repair it. This has the effect of qualifying the leaseholder's right of exclusive possession (see below), but only subject to certain conditions. The freeholder (or the freeholder's servants, such as agents or contractors) may enter only at reasonable times, and subject to the giving of reasonable notice. If these conditions are not met, the leaseholder is under no obligation to allow them in; and, even when the conditions are met, the landlord will be trespassing if he enters the property without the leaseholder's consent.

If the leaseholder refuses consent even though the time is reasonable and reasonable notice has been given, the landlord's remedy is to get a court order against the leaseholder compelling him to grant entry. It is probable, in such a case, that the landlord will seek, and get, an award of legal costs against the leaseholder.

Obligations of Freeholders

Exclusive possession and quiet enjoyment

The first and most important obligation on the freeholder, without which there would be no legal lease at all, is to respect the leaseholder's rights of 'exclusive possession' and 'quiet enjoyment'. Exclusive possession is the right to occupy the property and exclude others from it, especially the freeholder. Quiet enjoyment is another way of underlining the leaseholder's rights over the property: it means that the freeholder may not interfere with the leaseholder's use of the property provided that the terms of the lease are observed.

However, the leaseholder's right to quiet enjoyment applies only to breaches by the freeholder or the freeholder's servants such as agents or contractors. It is important to note this because the term is sometimes thought to mean that the freeholder must protect the leaseholder against any activity by anyone that interferes with his use of the property: this is not so. For example, if the freeholder carries out some activity elsewhere in the building that interferes with the leaseholder, the leaseholder's right to quiet enjoyment has been breached and he is entitled to redress unless the freeholder can show that the activity was necessary, for instance to comply with repairing obligations under the lease. But if the interference is caused by someone else, perhaps another leaseholder, the freeholder's obligation to provide quiet enjoyment has not been breached. And it is worth stressing in this connection that even if the other leaseholder is in breach of his lease, it is entirely up to the freeholder whether or not to take action: other leaseholders have no power to force the freeholder to deal with the situation.

The 'section 48' notice

Another important protection for leaseholders is found in section 48 of the Landlord and Tenant Act 1987. This was designed to deal with the situation in which freeholders seek to avoid their responsibilities by (to put it bluntly) doing a disappearing act. Sometimes freeholders would provide no address or telephone number or other means of contact, meaning that leaseholders were unable to hold the freeholder to his side of the agreement. Sections 47 and 48 therefore lay down that the freeholder must formally notify the leaseholder of his name and give an address within England and Wales at which he can be contacted, and that this information must be repeated on every demand for rent or service charge. This has proved especially valuable for leaseholders where the freeholder lives abroad, or is a company based abroad. It should be noted that the address does not have to be the freeholder's home, nor, if the freeholder is a company, its registered office; often it will be the address of a solicitor or property management company, or simply an accommodation address. But the key point is that any notice, or legal writ, is validly served if sent to that address, and the freeholder is not allowed to claim that it never came to his notice.

Good management

The freeholder is under an obligation to ensure that his management responsibilities are carried out in a proper and appropriate way. Leaseholders can take the freeholder to court if they believe they can show that they are not receiving the standard of management to which they are entitled. This may be an expensive and lengthy process but it better than the alternative, sometimes resorted to by leaseholders, of withholding rent or service charge. This is risky because, whatever the shortcomings of the freeholder's management, it puts the leaseholders in breach of the conditions of their lease and, as such, demonstrably in the wrong (even if the freeholder may be in the wrong as well).

It may be that leaseholders need more information so that they can decide whether the management is satisfactory. If so, there is power under the Leasehold Reform, Housing and Urban Development Act 1993 for a management audit to be demanded by an auditor acting on behalf of at least two-thirds of the qualifying leaseholders.

Qualifying leaseholders are those with leases of residential property originally granted for 21 years or more and requiring them to contribute to the cost of services. The purpose of the audit, the costs of which must be met by the leaseholders demanding it, is to discover whether the freeholder's duties are being carried out efficiently and effectively. The auditor is appointed by the leaseholders and must be either a qualified accountant or a qualified surveyor and must not live in the block concerned. The auditor has the right to demand papers from the freeholder and can go to court if they are not produced.

In extreme cases a leaseholder can use the Landlord and Tenant Act 1987 to force the appointment of a managing agent to run the block instead of the freeholder. The leaseholder must serve a notice telling the freeholder what the problems are and warning that unless they are put right a Leasehold Valuation Tribunal will be asked to appoint a managing agent. The LVT may make such an order if it satisfied that it is 'just and convenient'; the Act mentions, as specific examples where this may apply, cases where the freeholder is in breach of obligations under the lease and cases where service charges are being levied in respect of work of a poor standard or an unnecessarily high standard. It should be noted that this procedure, although in some ways it resembles the procedures for collective enfranchisement in Chapter Four, differs from them in that it can be carried out by any individual leaseholder; it does not require the consent of a majority. Note too that the procedure is not available if the freeholder is a local authority, a registered housing association, or the Crown.

A Recognised Tenants' Association (RTA), where there is one, has additional rights to be consulted about managing agents. The RTA can serve a notice requiring the freeholder to supply details of the managing agent and the terms of the management agreement. Recognised Tenants' Associations are more important, however, in connection with service charges, explained in the Chapter Three.

Leaseholders that are receiving a consistently poor or overpriced service may also wish to consider getting rid of the freeholder altogether by collective enfranchisement under the Leasehold Reform, Housing and Urban Development Act 1993 (see Chapter Four). In addition, there is now the right to manage without proving fault, which is contained in the Commonhold and Leasehold Reform Act 2002. This right to manage entitles leaseholders to take over management of a building without having to prove any fault on the part of a landlord or pay any compensation.

Assignment of Leases

One of the most important characteristics of a lease - in marked contrast to most tenancies - is that it may be bought and sold. Usually, the freeholder has no say in this: the leaseholder may sell to whom he likes for the best price he can get, provided that the purchaser agrees to be bound by the terms of the lease. It is, however, usual for the lease to lay down that the freeholder must be informed of any change of leaseholder.

What actually happens when a lease is sold is that the vendor agrees to transfer to the buyer his rights and obligations under the lease. This is called 'Assignment' of the lease. In some types of housing the freeholder has the right to intervene if an assignment is envisaged. The housing may, for instance, be reserved for a particular category of resident, such as the retired, so the freeholder is allowed to refuse consent to the assignment if the purchaser does not qualify. It was mentioned above that the assignee takes over all the rights and responsibilities attaching to the lease. This means, for instance, that he takes responsibility for any arrears of service charge. This is why purchasers' solicitors go to such lengths to ensure that no arrears or other unusual obligations are outstanding.

If the Lease Is Breached

If the terms of a lease are broken, the party offended against can go to court. This may be the leaseholder, for instance if the freeholder has failed to carry out a repair. But it is normally the freeholder that takes the leaseholder to court, for failure to pay ground rent or service charges or for breach of some other requirement.

It is for the court, if satisfied that the lease has been breached, to decide what to do. The normal remedy will be that the offending party must pay compensation and that the breach (if it is still continuing) must be put right. It is also likely that the loser will be obliged to pay the winner's legal costs as well as his own, a penalty often considerably more severe than the requirement to pay compensation.

A much more severe remedy open to the freeholder if the leaseholder is in breach is forfeiture of the lease. This means what it says: the lease is forfeited to the freeholder. Forfeiture is sometimes threatened by the more aggressive class of freeholder but the good news for leaseholders is that in practice courts have shown themselves loathe to grant it except in very serious cases.

Since the Housing Act 1996 took effect, as amended by the 2002 Commonhold and Leasehold Reform Act, forfeiture for unpaid service charges has been made more difficult for freeholders; this is covered in the next Chapter.

Where forfeiture is threatened for any reason other than failure to pay rent (which means the basic rent, not the service charge element), the freeholder must first serve a 'section 146 notice', so called after the relevant provision of the Law of Property Act 1925. In this he must state the nature of the breach of the lease, what action is required to put it right; if he wants monetary compensation for the breach, the notice must state this too. If the notice is not complied with, the freeholder may proceed to forfeit; but the leaseholder may go to court for relief from forfeiture.

The breach of the lease specified in the section 146 notice

must have occurred during the twelve years preceding the notice. For breaches older than this, no valid section 146 notice can be served and so forfeiture is not available. If the freeholder breaches the lease, the leaseholder can go to court (usually a Leasehold Valuation Tribunal) and seek an order requiring the freeholder to remedy the breach, to pay damages, or to do both. The commonest type of breach complained of by leaseholders is failure to carry out repairs, and this explains why action by leaseholders is less usual; they know that if they force the freeholder to do repairs the costs will be recovered through service charges. Legal action may be the best course if the dispute affects a single leaseholder: but if a number of leaseholders are involved they may well prefer to get rid of the freeholder altogether by collectively enfranchising their leases as described in Chapter Four.

3. MANAGING SERVICE CHARGES

Chapter 3

Service Charges and the Law

By far the commonest cause of dispute between leaseholders and freeholders is the provision of services and the levying of service charges. In extreme cases, leaseholders have been asked to contribute thousands of pounds towards the cost of major repairs, and have even suffered forfeiture of the lease if they are unable, or unwilling, to comply. Happily, such instances are rare; but even where the service charges are more moderate, they are often resented by leaseholders.

The landlord of rented property is expected to meet virtually all costs from the rent, whereas the freeholder of leasehold stock has no rent to fall back on (apart from the normally negligible ground rent). How, then, are major costs to be met when they arise? The answer, of course, is from the service charge, which is, therefore, of central importance to the management of leasehold property.

From the freeholder's point of view, the logic of service charges is impeccable. It is perfectly reasonable for freeholders to point out:

- that leaseholders benefit from the work because it has maintained or improved their homes; and
- that the fact that the work has been done means that leaseholders will get a better price when they come to sell; and
- that people that own their homes freehold have to find the money to meet costs of this kind.

In short, the purchase of a lease means the acceptance of a commitment to pay the appropriate share of costs.

But this does not mean that leaseholders have no scope to challenge or query service charges. Under sections 18 to 30 of the Landlord and Tenant Act 1985, as amended by the 2002 Commonhold and Leasehold Reform Act, they have extensive legal protection against improper or unreasonable charging by freeholders, and this is discussed later in the Chapter. First, however, we should look at how a typical service charge is made up.

What goes into a Service Charge?

The lease will say how often service charges are levied: typically, monthly, six-monthly or annually. It is usual to collect the ground rent at the same time, but this is usually a fairly small component of the bill. The service charge proper will normally consist of three elements.

- **The management fee** is the charge made by the freeholder, or the freeholder's agent, to cover the administrative cost of providing the service and collecting the charge. Usually it will be much the same amount from one year to the next, but if major works have occurred the management fee will usually be higher to cover the extra costs of appointing and supervising contractors; 15% of the cost of the works is a common figure.
- **Direct costs (routine expenditure)** cover costs such as the supply of electricity to communal areas, building insurance, and the like. Again, these costs are likely to be fairly constant from year to year, so leaseholders

know in advance roughly how much they are likely to have to pay.

- **Direct costs (exceptional expenditure)** cover costs that are likely to be irregular but heavy. They usually result from maintenance and repair, and it is because this component of the service charge is so unpredictable that it gives rise to so many problems. Where a house has been divided into leasehold flats, the freeholder's costs will usually be similar to what a normal homeowner would be obliged to pay; in other words, the costs may well be in the thousands (for a new roof, say) but are unlikely to be higher. Even so, a charge of £5000 for a new roof, even if divided between three or four flats, is still a major cost from the point of view of the individual leaseholder, especially if it is unexpected. The situation can be far worse in blocks of flats, where the costs of essential repair and maintenance may run into millions. Replacement of worn-out lifts, for example, is notoriously costly; and costs arising from structural defects are likely to be higher still.

Unreasonable Service Charges
General Principles
Sections 18 to 30 of the Landlord and Tenant Act 1985, as amended by the Landlord and Tenant Act 1987, and the Commonhold and Leasehold Reform Act 2002, grant substantial protection to leaseholders of residential property. This protection was introduced after complaints of exploitation by unscrupulous leaseholders, who were alleged to be carrying out unnecessary, or even fictitious, repairs at extravagant prices, whilst not providing the information that would have enabled leaseholders to query the bill. The effect of the Act is to require freeholders to provide

leaseholders with full Information about service charges and to consult them before expensive works are carried out.

A few leases, namely those granted under the right to buy by local authorities or registered housing associations, have some additional protection under the Housing Act 1985 (see below), but sections 18 to 30 apply to all residential leases where the service charge depends on how much the freeholder spends. They set out the key rules that freeholders must observe in order to recover the cost, including overheads, of 'services, repairs, maintenance or insurance', as well as the freeholder's costs of management.

It should be noted that failure by leaseholders to pay the service charge does not relieve the freeholder of the obligation to provide the services. The freeholder's remedy is to sue the leaseholder for the outstanding charges, or even to seek forfeiture of the lease (see below). Section 19 of the Act provides the key protection to leaseholders by laying down that service charges are recoverable only if they are 'reasonably incurred' and if the services or works are of a reasonable standard. This means that the charge:

- must relate to some form of 'service, repair, maintenance, or insurance' that the freeholder is required to provide under the lease;
- must be reasonable (that is, the landlord may not recover costs incurred unnecessarily or extravagantly);
- may cover overheads and management costs only if these too are reasonable.

In addition, the charge must normally be passed on to the leaseholders within 18 months of being incurred, and in some cases the freeholder must consult leaseholders before spending the money. These points are covered below.

The Housing Act 1996 (amended by the 2002 Commonhold

and Leasehold Reform Act 2002) gave leaseholders new powers to refer service charges to the Leasehold Valuation Tribunal (LVT). This is covered below (*Challenging Service Charges*).

Leasehold Valuation Tribunals operate throughout England and Wales. They are appointed jointly by the Lord Chancellor and (in England) the Environment Secretary and (in Wales) the Welsh Secretary. They perform a large number of quasi-judicial functions in relation to property, especially leasehold property.

Service Charge demands

Section 153 of the 2002 Commonhold and Leasehold Reform Act states that all demands for service charges must be accompanied by a summary of leaseholders rights and obligations. Accordingly, a leaseholder can withhold payment of charges if such a summary is not contained with a demand. Where a tenant withholds charges under section 153, the sections of a lease pertaining to payment of charges will not apply for the period for which the charge is withheld.

Sample summary of rights and obligations
Service Charges - Summary of tenants' rights and obligations

1. This summary, which briefly sets out your rights and obligations in relation to variable service charges, must by law accompany a demand for service charges. Unless a summary is sent to you with a demand, you may withhold the service charge. The summary does not give a full interpretation of the law and if you are in any doubt about your rights and obligations you should seek independent advice.

2. Your lease sets out your obligations to pay service charges to your landlord in addition to your rent. Service charges

are amounts payable for services, repairs, maintenance, improvements, insurance or the landlord's costs of management, to the extent that the costs have been reasonably incurred.

3. You have the right to ask a leasehold valuation tribunal to determine whether you are liable to pay service charges for services, repairs, maintenance, improvements, insurance or management. You may make a request before or after you have paid the service charge. If the tribunal determines that the service charge is payable, the tribunal may also determine-

   o who should pay the service charge and who it should be paid to;

   o the amount;

   o the date it should be paid by; and

   o how it should be paid.

   However, you do not have these rights where-

   o a matter has been agreed or admitted by you;

   o a matter has already been, or is to be, referred to arbitration or has been determined by arbitration and you agreed to go to arbitration after the disagreement about the service charge or costs arose; or a matter has been decided by a court.

4. If your lease allows your landlord to recover costs incurred or that may be incurred in legal proceedings as service charges, you may ask the court or tribunal, before which those proceedings were brought, to rule that your

landlord may not do so.

5. Where you seek a determination from a leasehold valuation tribunal, you will have to pay an application fee and, where the matter proceeds to a hearing, a hearing fee, unless you qualify for a waiver or reduction. The total fees payable will not exceed £500, but making an application may incur additional costs, such as professional fees, which you may also have to pay.

6. A leasehold valuation tribunal has the power to award costs, (currently not exceeding £500), against a party to any proceedings where-

   o it dismisses a matter because it is frivolous, vexatious or an abuse of process; or

   o it considers a party has acted frivolously, vexatiously, abusively, disruptively or unreasonably.
   The Upper Tribunal (Lands Chamber) has similar powers when hearing an appeal against a decision of a leasehold valuation tribunal.

7. If your landlord-

   o proposes works on a building or any other premises that will cost you or any other tenant more than £250, or

   o proposes to enter into an agreement for works or services which will last for more than 12 months and will cost you or any other tenant more than £100 in any 12 month accounting period, then your contribution will be limited to these amounts unless your landlord has properly consulted on the proposed works or agreement or a leasehold valuation tribunal has agreed that consultation is not required. You have the right to apply to a leasehold valuation tribunal to ask it to determine whether your lease should be varied on the grounds that it does not make satisfactory provision in respect of the calculation of a service charge payable under the lease.

8. You have the right to write to your landlord to request a written summary of the costs which make up the service charges. The summary must-

    o   cover the last 12 month period used for making up the accounts relating to the service charge ending no later than the date of your request, where the accounts are made up for 12 month periods; or

    o   cover the 12 month period ending with the date of your request, where the accounts are not made up for 12 month periods.

    o   The summary must be given to you within 1 month of your request or 6 months of the end of the period to which the summary relates whichever is the later.

9. You have the right, within 6 months of receiving a written summary of costs, to require the landlord to provide you with reasonable facilities to inspect the accounts, receipts and other documents supporting the summary and for taking copies or extracts from them.

10. You have the right to ask an accountant or surveyor to carry out an audit of the financial management of the premises containing your dwelling, to establish the obligations of your landlord and the extent to which the service charges you pay are being used efficiently. It will depend on your circumstances whether you can exercise this right alone or only with the support of others living in the premises. You are strongly advised to seek independent advice before exercising this right.

11. Your lease may give your landlord a right of re-entry or forfeiture where you have failed to pay charges which are properly due under the lease. However, to exercise this right, the landlord must meet all the legal requirements and obtain a court order. A court order will only be granted if you have admitted you are liable to pay the amount or it is finally determined by a court, tribunal or by arbitration that the amount is due. The court has a wide discretion in granting such an order and it will take into account all the circumstances of the case.

Consultation with Leaseholders

Section 20 of the LTA 1985, which is the area of the Act dealing with the landlords obligation to consult leaseholders over both major expenditure, and also before entering into long-term agreements for the provision of services, has been substituted by section 151 of the 2002 Commonhold and Leasehold Reform Act, which came into effect on 31st October 2003.

Major works and long term agreements

Section 151 provides extra protection where the cost of works is more than £250 per leaseholder. Therefore, if a landlord owns a block of 20 flats and wishes to spend £8,000 on repairs, the limit above which he will have to legally consult is £5,000. Costs above this level are irrecoverable (except, sometimes, when the works are urgent) unless the freeholder has taken steps to inform and consult tenants. If the leaseholders are represented by a recognised tenants' association, i.e. formally constituted and recognised by the landlord as well as leaseholders, they must also receive copies of the consultation notices along with individual leaseholders.

In relation to long term agreements, these are agreements over 12 months. Such agreements may be those for servicing lifts. They do not include contracts of employment. The consultation limit for long term contracts is now £100 per person per annum. If the amount exceeds this then consultation must be carried out. The steps in the consultation procedure are as follows:

Landlords statement of why works are necessary. There is a requirement for the landlord to state why he considers the works or the agreement to be necessary. This is defined by a 1-month period within which the landlord must take account of all responses from leaseholders. All letters and responses have to be prepared in accordance with the requirements of the Act (2002 CLRA).

Estimates. Following this initial stage, at least two estimates must be obtained, of which at least one must be from someone wholly unconnected with the freeholder (obviously a building firm that the freeholder owns or works for is not 'wholly unconnected'; nor is the freeholder's managing agent).

Notification to leaseholders The freeholder must either display a copy of the estimates somewhere they are likely to be seen by everyone liable to pay the service charge, or (preferably) send copies to everyone liable to pay the service charge.

Consultation The notification must describe the works to be carried out and must seek comments and observations, giving a deadline for replies and an address in the UK to which they may be sent. The deadline must be at least a month after the notice was sent or displayed.

Freeholder's response The freeholder must 'have regard' to any representations received. This does not mean, of course, that the freeholder must do what the leaseholders say. It does mean, however, that the freeholder must consider any comments received, and good freeholders often demonstrate that they have done so by sending a reasoned reply.

Therefore, a consultation period will usually be a minimum of 60 days from notification to instructions to carry out works.

If a service charge is challenged in court for failure to follow these procedures, it is a defence for the freeholder to show that the works were urgent. However, the court would need to be satisfied that the urgency was genuine and that the freeholder behaved reasonably in the circumstances.

Section 151 is important because it gives the leaseholders notification of any unusual items in the offing and gives them an opportunity to raise any concerns and objections. If the leaseholder has any reservations at all, it is vital that they be put before the freeholder at this stage. It is highly unlikely, in the event of legal action later, that the court will support a leaseholder who raised no objection until the bill arrived. It is common for freeholders and their agents to fail to comply with the requirements of section 151. This comment applies not only where the freehold is owned by an individual or a relatively small organisation (where mistakes might be more understandable) but also where the freeholder is a large, well resourced body like a local authority. As a result leaseholders are often paying service charges that are not due, so all leaseholders should, before paying a service charge containing unusual items, ensure that section 151, if it applies, has been scrupulously followed. If not, they can refuse to pay.

Other Protection for Leaseholders
Grant-aided works:
If the freeholder has received a grant towards the cost of carrying out the works, the amount must be deducted from the service charge levied on leaseholders.

Late charging
Service charge bills may not normally include costs incurred more than eighteen months earlier. The freeholder may, however, notify leaseholders within the eighteen month period that they will have to pay a certain cost, and then bill them later. This might happen if, for instance, the freeholder is in dispute with a contractor about the level of a bill or the standard of work.

Pre-charging
Sometimes a lease will contain a provision allowing the freeholder to make a charge to cover future costs besides those already incurred. This practice, which is perfectly lawful in itself, may be in the interests of the leaseholders by spreading over a longer period the cost of major works. It is, however, subject to the same requirement of reasonableness.

Court costs
Section 20C of the LTA 1985, provides protection against a

specific abuse of the service charge system by freeholders. Previously, freeholders tended to regard their legal costs as part of the process of managing the housing and thus as recoverable from leaseholders. Such an attitude is not necessarily unreasonable. For example, if the freeholder is suing a builder for poor work, he is, in effect, acting on behalf of all the leaseholders and it is fair that they should pay any legal costs. But suppose the freeholder were involved in legal proceedings against one of the leaseholders: if the leaseholder lost, he would probably be ordered to pay the freeholder's costs as well as his own; but if the freeholder lost, and had to pay both his own and the leaseholder's costs, he could simply, under the previous law, recover the money as part of the management element in the service charge. This meant that the freeholder was able to pursue legal action against leaseholders without fear of heavy legal costs in the event of defeat, the very factor that deters most people from resorting to law.

To prevent this, section 20C allows leaseholders to seek an order that the freeholder's legal costs must not be counted towards service charges. Such an order is available in respect of not only court proceedings but also proceedings before a Leasehold Valuation Tribunal, the Lands Tribunal, or an arbitral tribunal. An application for an order may be made by the leaseholder concerned in the case to the court or tribunal hearing it. If the case has finished, any leaseholder may apply for an order to the Lands Tribunal if the case was heard there, to any Leasehold Valuation Tribunal if it was heard by a LVT, or otherwise to the county court.

Service charges held on trust
Section 42 of the Landlord and Tenant Act 1987 (as amended by the 2002 CLRA) further strengthened the position of

leaseholders by laying down that the freeholder, or the freeholder's agent, must hold service charge monies in a suitable trust fund that will ensure that the money is protected and cannot be seized by the freeholder's creditors if the freeholder goes bankrupt or into liquidation. However, public sector freeholders, notably local authorities and registered housing associations, are exempt from this requirement.

Insurance

Usually the lease provides for the landlord to arrange the insurance of the building (not the contents) and charge the cost as a service charge. This is the normal arrangement for buildings divided into flats, since it is important that there should be one single policy covering all risks to the building as a whole. It is normally recovered as part of the service charges and therefore the cost of the insurance may be challenged before or verified by the LVT in the usual way.

Where a service charge consists of or includes an amount payable for insurance, an individual leaseholder or the secretary of a recognised tenants' association may ask the landlord for a written summary of the policy or an opportunity to inspect and take copies of the policy.

The request must be made in writing and the landlord must comply within 21 days of receiving it.

• where the request is for a written summary, the summary must show:

– the sum for which the property is insured;

– the name of the insurer;

– the risks covered in the policy.

The landlord can only be required to provide the summary once in each insurance period (usually a year).

• Where the request is for sight of the policy, the landlord must provide reasonable access for inspection of the policy and any other relevant documents which provide evidence of payment, including receipts, and facilities for copying them. Alternatively, the request may be for the landlord to provide the copies of the policy and specified documents himself and to send them to the leaseholder or association or arrange for them to be collected.

'Period of Grace'

When a dwelling is sold under the right to buy by a local authority or non-charitable housing association, the purchaser is given an estimate of service charges for the following five years. This estimate is the maximum recoverable during that time. Some purchasers under the right to buy have, however, had a very rude shock when the five year period of grace expires - see *Exceptionally High Service Charges* below.

The role of a recognised tenants' association

The tenants who are liable to pay for the provision of services may, if they wish, form a recognised tenants' association (RTA) under section 29 of the Landlord and Tenant Act 1985. Note that leaseholders count as tenants for this purpose (see Chapter One, where it explained that legally the two terms are interchangeable). If the freeholder refuses to give a notice recognising the RTA, it may apply for recognition to any member of the local Rent Assessment Committee panel ('Rent Assessment Committee' is the official term for a Leasehold Valuation Tribunal when it is carrying out certain functions, not otherwise relevant to leaseholders, under the Rent Act 1977).

An important benefit of having a RTA is that it has the right, at the beginning of the consultation process, to recommend persons or organisations that should be invited to submit estimates. However, the freeholder is under no obligation to accept these recommendations.

Another advantage is that the RTA can, whether the

freeholder likes it or not, appoint a qualified surveyor to advise on matters relating to service charges. The surveyor has extensive rights to inspect the freeholder's documentation and take copies, and can enforce these rights in court if necessary.

Statement of accounts to leaseholders

Under section 152 of the Commonhold and Leasehold Reform Act 2002, which has substituted s.21 of the Landlord and Tenant Act 1985, a landlord must supply a statement of accounts to each tenant by who service charges are payable, in relation to each accounting period. These accounts deal with:

a) Service charges of the tenant and the tenants of dwellings associated with his dwelling
b) Relevant costs relating to those service charges
c) The aggregate amount standing to the credit of the tenant and the tenants of those dwellings at the beginning and the end of the accounting period in question.

This statement of account must be supplied to the tenant not later than six months after the accounting period. A certificate of a qualified auditor must be supplied and, in addition, a summary of the rights and obligations of the tenant in relation to service charges must be supplied.

Challenging Service Charges

The Landlord and Tenant Act not only allows leaseholders to take action against unreasonable behaviour by the freeholder; it also enables them to take the initiative. This is done in two ways: by giving leaseholders rights to demand information, and by allowing them to challenge the reasonableness of the charge.

Right to require information

Leaseholders have the right to ask freeholders for a written summary of costs counting towards the service charge. This is contained within s.22 of the Landlord and Tenant Act 1985, as amended by s.154 of the Commonhold and Leasehold Reform Act 2002. Such a summary must cover either the twelve months up to the point where it was requested or, if accounts are drawn up annually, the last complete twelve-month accounting period before the request was made. It must be sent to the leaseholder within 21 days of the request or within six months of the end of the period it covers, whichever is the later. Failure to provide it without reasonable excuse is a criminal offence carrying a maximum fine of £2500.

The law lays down some minimum requirements for the summary. It must:

- cover all the costs incurred during the twelve months it covers, even if they were included in service charge bills of an earlier or later period (see above for late charging and pre-charging);
- show how the costs incurred by the freeholder are reflected in the service charges paid, or to be paid, by leaseholders;
- say whether it includes any work covered by a grant (see above);
- distinguish: (a) those costs incurred for which the freeholder was not billed during the period; (b) those for which he was billed and did not pay; (c) those for which he paid bills.

If it covers five or more dwellings, the summary must, in addition, be certified by a qualified accountant as being a fair summary, complying with the Act, and supported by appropriate documentation.

The purpose of section 22, as amended, is to put leaseholders in a position to challenge their service charges. After receiving the summary, the leaseholder has six months in which to ask the freeholder to make facilities available so that he can inspect the documents supporting the summary (bills, receipts, and so on) and take copies or extracts. The freeholder must respond within a month and make the facilities available within the two months following that; the inspection itself must be free, although the freeholder can make a reasonable charge for the copies and extracts. Failure to provide these facilities, like failure to supply the summary, is punishable by a fine of up to £2500.

Very similar rules apply where the lease allows, or requires, the freeholder to take out insurance against certain contingencies, such as major repair, and to recover the premiums through the service charge. This is not unreasonable in itself and will, indeed, often be in the interests of leaseholders. The danger is, however, that the freeholder, knowing that the premiums are, in effect, being paid by someone else, has no incentive to shop around for the best deal. Section 30A of the Landlord and Tenant Act 1985 therefore lays down that leaseholders, or the secretary of the recognised tenants' association if there is one, may ask the freeholder for information about the policy. Failure to supply it, or to make facilities to inspect relevant documents available if requested to do so, is an offence incurring a fine of up to £2500.

It must be acknowledged that the rules allowing leaseholders to require information about service charges are, particularly in view of the £2500 fines, fairly onerous from the freeholder's point of view.

It is the purpose of this book to inform leaseholders of their rights, not to make life difficult for freeholders: nevertheless, it must be admitted that if leaseholders wish to pursue a policy of confronting freeholders, and to cause them as much trouble as possible, sections 21, 22, and 30A offer plenty of scope.

Challenging the reasonableness of a service charge
Any leaseholder liable to pay a service charge, and for that matter any freeholder levying one, may refer the charge to a Leasehold Valuation Tribunal to determine its reasonableness. This may be done at any time, even when the service in question is merely a proposal by the freeholder (for instance, for future major works).

But the LVT will not consider a service charge if:
- it has already been approved by a court; or
- if the leaseholder has agreed to refer it to arbitration; or
- if the leaseholder has agreed it.

The first of these exceptions is obvious and the second is unlikely to apply very often. The third one is the problem: leaseholders should be careful, in their dealings with freeholders, to say or do nothing that could be taken to imply that they agree with any service charge that is in any way doubtful.

The LVT will consider:
- whether the freeholder's costs of services, repairs, maintenance, insurance, or management are reasonably incurred;
- whether the services or works are of a reasonable standard; and
- whether any payment required in advance is reasonable.

The fees for application to a LVT can be obtained from the LVT and will usually change annually. Appeal against a LVT decision is not to the courts but to the Lands Tribunal.

By section 19 of the Landlord and Tenant Act 1985, any service charge deemed unreasonable by the LVT is irrecoverable by the freeholder. The determination of service charges by the LVT also plays an important part in the rules governing the use of forfeiture to recover service charges. .

Forfeiture for Unpaid Service Charges

Forfeiture was mentioned at the end of Chapter Two. Briefly, it is the right of the freeholder to take possession of the property if the leaseholder breaches the lease.

By section 81 of the Housing Act 1996, as amended by the 2002 Commonhold and Leasehold Reform Act, forfeiture for an unpaid service charge is available to the freeholder only if:

- the leaseholder has agreed the charge; or
- the charge has been upheld through arbitration or by a court or Leasehold Valuation Tribunal.

Regarding the first of these, it is necessary only to reiterate the warning to leaseholders to say or do nothing that could possibly be construed as representing their agreement to any service charge about whose legitimacy they have the slightest doubt.

Regarding the second, it should be noted that where the leaseholder has not agreed the service charge, court proceedings or formal arbitration are necessary before the freeholder can forfeit the lease.

Exceptionally High Service Charges

So far this Chapter has focused on service charges of normal proportions that, however unforeseen and unwelcome they may be, should be within the means of the great majority of leaseholders. A minority of leaseholders, however, face the much more serious problem of consistently very high service charges.

Where the cause is sharp practice by the freeholder, or failure to observe the legal requirements, the leaseholder can look for protection to the Landlord and Tenant Act as described above. Often, however, the freeholder is not to blame: rather, the problem is that the work is genuinely necessary and unavoidably expensive. In this situation, and provided the landlord carefully follows the procedures laid down, the Landlord and Tenant Act offers no protection.

In what sort of housing is this most likely to occur? It is more likely to affect flats than houses because flats tend to contain potentially very expensive components such as lifts or communal arrangements for heating or ventilation. They are also more likely to have been built using construction methods or designs in vogue at one time but since found to lead to serious maintenance problems and high costs, whereas house building seems to be innately conservative and resistant to innovation: for instance, many blocks of flats contain asbestos, but very few houses.

All these problems apply to flats in general, but there is an additional problem with blocks of flats owned by local authorities and housing associations: namely that, unlike blocks of flats developed by commercial owners for sale, they are likely to combine rented properties, let to periodic tenants in the usual way, with leasehold properties, sold at some point in the past under the right to buy or some similar scheme. These 'mixed managed' blocks present special problems for both categories of resident as well as the freeholder.

Clearly, there is no satisfactory way to resolve this problem. In a privately developed block, occupied wholly by leaseholders, the freeholder might possibly be prevailed upon to delay the repairs for a time if the leaseholders are prepared to put up with the poor conditions; but the Council can hardly be expected to take the same view when most of the residents are periodic tenants. Both the Council and the periodic tenants are likely to argue that the leaseholders are being asked to do no more than they agreed to do when they bought their leases.

All this book can do is warn prospective leaseholders of the serious problems that can arise in a minority of cases, and suggest some of the questions that they should ask before signing the lease.

What is the condition of the building as a whole?

No one would buy a house, or an individual flat, without looking closely at its condition and estimating how much money it may need to have spent on it. But, when a flat is being bought, whether it is purpose-built or a conversion, it is equally important to look at the entire building of which it forms a part. The vendor should be asked for copies of past service charges, the freeholder should be asked whether major work is likely in the foreseeable future and what it is likely to cost, and an independent surveyor should be asked to report.

What is the leaseholder's liability?

The lease will specify what the leaseholder must pay for. Sometimes it will require him to contribute to things from which he does not benefit. For example, it is common for even ground floor leaseholders to be expected to contribute to the costs of the lifts; and some leaseholders, having paid out of their own pockets to replace their windows, are outraged to discover, when the freeholder has the windows of the whole block renewed, that they are required to pay a share of the cost.

Provisions such as these are much resented by many leaseholders, who argue that they are unfair; but the time to object to such unfairness is before signing the lease, not many years later when the bills come in. It is therefore essential that anyone proposing to enter into a lease should first consult a solicitor.

Is there a 'period of grace' or other safeguard?

Right to buy leases contain an estimate of service charges for five years following the sale and that is the maximum that the Council may charge. Many purchasers, reassured by this, have signed the lease without paying much attention to the likely level of service charges thereafter, expecting perhaps to have sold at a profit and moved on before the five years expire. If so, they have been reminded of what many people forgot during the 1980s: that property prices can go down as well as up. In short, it is unwise to rely on a 'period of grace' to provide anything other than short-term relief; and in particular it is unwise to speculate on the future behaviour of the housing market.

What are the prospects for resale?

Traditionally, the homeowner's last resort in the face of overwhelming financial problems is to sell up in the expectation that the proceeds will suffice to pay off the mortgage, settle other outstanding debts such as service charges, and still leave something over. A stagnant property market has upset many calculations of this kind, but selling up remains an option if the mortgage is appreciably less than the value of the property, and if the service charges are not too high. So it is important to assess the saleability of the dwelling by asking whether future purchasers are likely to be put off by anything about the flat itself or the block and district to which it belongs, and above all whether mortgage lenders are likely to look on it favourably.

Ground rent demands

Ground rents are charged by freeholders, to leaseholders and are usually fixed annual charges, and can vary greatly. Under section 166 of the Coonmonhold and Leasehold Reform Act 2002, it is the duty of all landlords to give formal notice of a demand for ground rents. A sample notice is contained below

.

FORM OF RENT DEMAND NOTICE

COMMONHOLD AND LEASEHOLD REFORM ACT 2002, SECTION 166

NOTICE TO LONG LEASEHOLDERS OF RENT DUE

To *(insert name(s) of leaseholder(s)):*

This notice is given in respect of *(address of premises to which the long lease relates)*

It requires you to pay rent of £.............on *(insert date)* (note 2)...............

This rent is payable in respect of the period *(state period)*

[In accordance with the terms of your lease the amount of £.... is/was due on *(insert date.............*

on which rent due in accordance with the lease).] (note 3)

Payment should be made to *(insert name of landlord(s) or if payment to be made to an agent, name of agent)* at *(insert address)*

This notice is given by *(insert name of landlord(s) and, if not given above, address)*

NOTES FOR LEASEHOLDERS

Read this notice carefully. It sets out the amount of rent due from you and the date by which you must pay it. You are advised to seek help immediately, if you cannot pay, or dispute the amount,. Those who can help you include a citizens' advice bureau, a housing advice centre, a law centre and a solicitor. Show this notice and a copy of your lease to whoever helps you.

The landlord may be able to claim additional sums from you if you do not pay by the date specified in this notice. You have the right to challenge the reasonableness of any additional sums at a leasehold valuation tribunal.

Section 167 of the Commonhold and Leasehold Reform Act 2002 and regulations made under it prevent your landlord from forfeiting your lease for non-payment of rent, service charges or administration charges (or a combination of them) if the amount owed is £350 or less, or none of the unpaid amount has been outstanding for more than three years.

NOTES FOR LANDLORDS

I. If you send this notice by post, address it to the leaseholder at the dwelling in respect of which the payment is due, unless he has notified you in writing of a different address in England and Wales at which he wishes to be given notices under section 166 of the Commonhold and Leasehold Reform Act 2002.

2. This date must not be *either* less than 30 days or more than 60 days after the day on which this notice is given *or* before that on which the leaseholder would have been liable to make the payment in accordance with the lease.

3. Include this statement only if the date for payment is not the same as the date determined in accordance with the lease.

4

PURCHASING THE FREEHOLD AND EXTENDING THE LEASE

Chapter 4

Purchasing the Freehold and Extension of Leases

Enfranchising or extending leases

The sale of the freehold to leaseholders is called 'Enfranchisement'. Extending a lease means to extend it from its existing term, i.e. make longer.

The following are reasons for enfranchising or extending leases.

- a lease is a wasting asset and with every year that passes it gets shorter. Eventually, a flat will become unmortgagable and difficult to sell. Silly as it may sound, a lease with less than 80 years left to run is now regarded as being "short" and even leases with 80 to 85 years left may be difficult to sell

- a lease extension will preserve, and perhaps even increase, the value of a flat

- if leaseholders enfranchise they can grant themselves extended leases

- many existing leases do not satisfy mortgage lenders' current requirements. If leaseholders enfranchise they can rewrite leases to overcome that problem

- leaseholders may be unhappy with the management of their building. If they enfranchise they can take control of the management

LEASEHOLD REFORM, HOUSING AND URBAN DEVELOPMENT ACT 1993

The area of leasehold enfranchisement has attracted a plethora of media and academic interest since its formal introduction in 1967 and has been amended and expanded over the past four decades. The right of long leaseholders to buy their landlord's interest outright or acquire an extended lease term, is unique to England and Wales and, perhaps unsurprisingly, has led to a number of legal challenges over the years. Landlords and tenants alike are anxious to protect their respective property interests in a market that shows no sign of abating. Consequently, this area of the law is continually evolving.

In general terms, the legislation confers two distinct rights: to purchase the freehold, either individually in relation to leasehold houses, or collectively for a block of flats, or to seek a lease extension. Although these rights are curtailed by the statutory tests for qualification, changes to the legislation, introduced by the Commonhold and Leasehold Reform Act 2002, have made it easier than ever for leaseholders to make a claim.

The requirement that leaseholders must have occupied the property in question for a period of two years (the so-called residence requirement) has largely been swept away and replaced by a new, two year ownership test. Indeed, in the case of a collective enfranchisement, even the ownership requirement has been removed. Likewise, qualification tests based on the property's ratable values and rent have gone, with the result that higher value houses, for example, may now enfranchise.

The Collective Right to enfranchise
What is it?

This gives the right for tenants of flats acting together to purchase the freehold and any headleases of their building. In order for the building to qualify under the Act, it must:
• be an independent building or be a part of a building which is capable of independent development; and
• contain two or more flats held by qualifying tenants; and
• have at least two thirds of the flats held by qualifying tenants.
In order to be a qualifying tenant you must have a long lease which means a lease which, when originally granted, was for a term of more than 21 years. However, you must not own three or more flats in the building. You cannot be a qualifying tenant if you hold a business lease.

Notwithstanding the above, the building will not qualify if:
• it comprises four or less units and has a "resident freeholder";
• more than 25% of the internal floor space (excluding common parts) is used for non-residential purposes;
• the building is part of an operational railway.

How do I prepare for a claim?

Any qualifying tenant can give a notice to his landlord or the managing agent requiring details of the various legal interests in the block. This notice places no commitment on the tenant but the response to the notice should provide the tenant with the information necessary for him to ascertain whether the building contains a sufficient number of qualifying tenants for it to qualify.

Having established that the building qualifies, it is then advisable to ascertain whether you have a sufficient number of tenants who want to participate, both for the purpose of qualifying for enfranchisement and for the purpose of being able to finance the acquisition. In order to qualify for enfranchisement, you need to establish that the number of participating tenants comprises not less than one half of all the flats in the building. However, if there are only two flats in the building then both must participate.

When you have established that the building qualifies and that there is a sufficient number of qualifying tenants who wish to participate, then there are five further practical steps which should be taken before embarking on the enfranchisement procedure.

First, you need to establish what it is going to cost by obtaining a valuation. In simple terms, the price to be paid by the participating tenants to purchase the freehold of the building is the aggregate of:

- The building's investment value to the freeholder-the capitalised value of his ground rents and the value of his reversion (being the present freehold vacant possession value deferred for the unexpired term of the lease).
- One half of the marriage value-the increased value attributable to the freehold by virtue of the participating tenants being able to grant themselves extended leases at nil premium and a peppercorn rent. The marriage value attributable to a lease held by a participating tenant will be deemed to be nil if that lease has an unexpired term of more than 80 years at the date that the initial notice is given.
- Compensation for loss of value of other property owned by the freeholder, including development value consequent to the severance of the building from that other property.

The valuation date is the date that the claim notice is given.

Value added to the flat of a participating tenant by tenant's improvements is disregarded in the valuation.

For the purposes of calculating price, the tenants should take the advice of a properly qualified surveyor or valuer with experience in the field of enfranchisement and knowledge of the market.

In addition to the price and the participating tenants' own legal costs and valuation fees, the claimants will be required to reimburse the freeholder his legal costs and valuation fees.

Secondly, the participators will need to establish how to finance the cost of acquisition. It may, for example, be necessary for a number of participating tenants to seek a further advance from a Building Society or Bank. In particular, the participators will want to decide who is to finance the purchase of the non-participators' flats and on what basis.

Thirdly, it will be necessary to establish what vehicle the participating tenants should use in order to buy the freehold and how they will establish and regulate the relationship between themselves. In most cases, this is likely to be through a company structure, although in some circumstances a trust might be more appropriate. It should be noted that the participating tenants do not all have to have equal shares, so that the proportion of the shareholdings will be a matter for negotiation between them.

The 2002 Act provides for collective claims to be made through the mechanism of a Right to Enfranchise (RTE) company. However those provisions have never been brought into force and it is unlikely that they will be.

Fourthly, the participating tenants should seek advice to establish whether there are tax implications to the transaction, both in relation to their individual positions and in relation to the vehicle chosen to buy the freehold.

Finally, the collective enfranchisement legislation provides no guidance or controls on the way in which the participating tenants should work together in order to acquire the freehold. Since the purchase may well involve substantial sums of money and is likely to take time to complete and, during this time, the participating tenants will be heavily reliant on each other for the performance of tasks within strict limits, it is strongly advised that, before embarking on a claim, the participating tenants should enter into a formal agreement (called a participation agreement) in order to regulate the relationship between them during the course of the claim.

How is the claim made?

It is important to be aware that most of the time limits imposed on the procedural stages of the claim are strict and a failure to do something within the required time frame can have dire consequences for the defaulter. It is therefore essential that, by the time you reach the next stage of the procedure, you are well organised and backed by expert professional advice.

The reason for this is that the next procedural step is the service by the participating tenants on the landlord of what the Act calls the initial notice – the notice which claims the right to collective enfranchisement. Costs start to run against the tenants from the time they serve the initial notice. Amongst other things this notice must specify:

• the extent of the property to be acquired – supported by a plan;
• full particulars of all the qualifying tenants in the building –
not just the participating tenants;
• the price being offered for the freehold – the offer should be
genuine;
• the name and address of the nominee purchaser – the person or

company nominated by the participating tenants to conduct the negotiations and to buy the freehold on their behalf;

• the date by which the freeholder must give his counter-notice, being a date not less than two months from the date of the service of the initial notice.

The freeholder is likely to respond with a procedural notice requiring the participating tenants to deduce title. The freeholder's valuer is also likely to inspect the building for the purpose of carrying out a valuation.

Within the period specified in the initial notice, the freeholder must serve his counter-notice. First and foremost, this must state whether or not the claim is admitted. If it is not, then the participating tenants must decide if they wish to dispute the rejection through the courts.

There are circumstances where the freeholder can resist a claim on the ground of redevelopment. If the claim is admitted, then the counter-notice must state, amongst other things:

• which of the proposals contained in the initial notice are acceptable;
• which of the proposals contained in the initial notice are not acceptable and what are the freeholder's counter-proposals – particularly on price;
• whether the freeholder wants a leaseback on any units in the building not held by a qualifying tenant (for example, a flat subject to a short term tenancy or a commercial unit).
• compensation for loss in value of other property owned by the freeholder, including development value consequent to sale

Disputes

If any terms of acquisition (including the price) remain in dispute after two months following the date of the counter-notice, then either party can apply to the leasehold valuation tribunal for the matter in dispute to be determined.

This application must be made within six months following the date of the counter-notice or the claim is lost. Most claims are settled by negotiation. If a leasehold valuation tribunal is required to make a determination, then there is a right to appeal that decision to the Lands Tribunal if permission is given to do so.

Completion

Once the terms of acquisition have been agreed or determined by the leasehold valuation tribunal, then the matter reverts to a conveyancing transaction with the parties entering into a sale contract on the terms agreed or determined and thence to completion.

If the matter proceeds to completion, then the participating tenants, through their nominee purchaser, will become the freeholder of the building, subject to the various flat leases. In effect, the participating tenants will replace the existing freeholder. This will put them in a position to grant themselves extended leases.

There may be taxation consequences on granting an extended lease, particularly for second home owners. There will also be responsibilities. The participating tenants will become responsible for the management of the building and the administration of the service charge account in accordance with the covenants in the original leases.

If the nominee purchaser is a company, all participators will be shareholders and some will be officers of that company. These are all matters on which clear professional advice will be needed. It is important to note that an individual tenant has no right to become a participating tenant – even if he is a qualifying tenant. It is a matter for the tenants to resolve between themselves. You can always ask to be allowed to join in, but you will have no remedy if refused. If a group does form without you – and does not need you – you may well find yourself left out.

However, if you are left out, that need not necessarily be the end of the road. This is because of the second major innovation that was introduced by the 1993 Act – the individual right to acquire a new lease.

The individual right to extend leases
What is it?

The individual right to a statutory lease extension applies to all qualifying tenants of flats. The condition is that you must be the tenant of a flat which you hold on a long lease (i.e. a lease for an original term in excess of 21 years). Furthermore, you must have owned the lease for at least two years before the date of the claim. For the purpose of the lease extension, There is no limit to the number of flats you may own in the building and you may extend any or all of them provided that the conditions are met. However, you cannot be a qualifying tenant if you hold a business lease.

Prior to the 2002 Act, the personal representatives of a deceased tenant had no rights to make a claim, even where the deceased tenant was able to fulfil the qualifying conditions. However, such personal representatives can now make a claim provided that the right is exercised within a period of two years from the date of grant of probate.

What do I get?

If you qualify, then you will be entitled to acquire a new extended lease in substitution for your existing lease. This extended lease will be for a term expiring 90 years after the end of the current lease and will reserve a peppercorn rent throughout the term.

Broadly, the lease will otherwise be on the same terms as the existing lease but the landlord will have certain additional redevelopment rights, exercisable within 12 months before the expiration of the current lease term and within 5 years before the expiration of the extended lease.

The price

The price to be paid for the new lease will be the aggregate of: •
the diminution in value of the landlord's interest in the flat, consequent on the grant of the extended lease; being the capitalised value of the landlord's ground rent and the value of his reversion (being the
present near-freehold vacant possession value deferred for the unexpired lease term);

• 50% of the marriage value (the additional value released by the tenant's ability to merge the extended lease with the existing lease) must be paid to the landlord although the marriage value will be deemed to be nil if the existing lease has an unexpired term of more than 80 years at the date of the claim;
• compensation for loss in value of other property owned by the freeholder, including development value, consequent on the grant of the new lease
.

The valuation date is the date of the claim notice. In addition to the price and the tenant's own legal costs and valuation fees, you will also be required to reimburse the freeholder his legal costs and valuation fees.

How do I claim?

The procedure to be followed is very similar to that for collective enfranchisement. It is therefore important to be aware that most of the time limits imposed on the procedural stages of the claim are strict and a failure to do something within the required time frame can have dire consequences for the defaulter.

The qualifying tenant can serve a preliminary notice to obtain information. Thereafter, he serves his notice of claim (in this case called the tenant's notice of claim) which amongst other things needs to state:

- a description of the flat – but not necessarily with a plan;
- sufficient particulars to establish that the lease qualifies;
- the premium being offered – it must be a bona fide offer;
- the terms of the new lease;
- the date by which the landlord must give the counter-notice, being a date not less than two months from the date of service of the tenant's notice.

The landlord is likely to respond with a procedural notice requiring payment of a deposit (equal to 10% of the premium being offered) and asking the tenant to deduce title. The landlord's valuer is also likely to inspect the flat for the purpose of carrying out a valuation.

Within the period specified in the tenant's notice, the landlord must serve his counter-notice. First and foremost, this must state whether or not the claim is admitted. If it is not, then the tenant must decide if he wishes to dispute the rejection through the courts. However, unlike a collective enfranchisement claim where the nominee purchaser makes the application to the court in these circumstances, in the case of the statutory lease extension, it is the landlord who makes the application if he has refused the claim.

Enfranchisement

There are circumstances where the landlord can resist a claim on the ground of redevelopment. If the claim is admitted, then the counter-notice must state, amongst
other things:

• which of the proposals contained in the tenant's notice are acceptable;
• which of the proposals contained in the tenant's notice are not acceptable and what are the landlord's counter-proposals – particularly
the premium.

Disputes

If either the terms of the lease or the premium remain in dispute after two months following the date of the counter-notice, then either party can apply to the leasehold valuation tribunal for the matter in dispute to be determined.

This application must be made within six months following the date of the counter-notice or the claim is lost. Most claims are settled by negotiation. If a leasehold valuation tribunal
is required to make a determination, then there is a right to appeal that decision to the Lands Tribunal if permission is given to do so

Completion

Once the terms of the lease and the premium have been agreed or determined   by   the   leasehold valuation   tribunal,   then   the matter reverts to a conveyancing transaction with the parties proceeding to completion of the new lease.

The tenant can withdraw at any time and there are provisions for the tenant's notice to be considered withdrawn if certain strict time limits are not met by the tenant. As in collective enfranchisement, the tenant is on risk as to costs as from the date of his tenant's notice so it is essential to be prepared and to be properly advised before starting down the road to an extension.

A tenant's notice is capable of being assigned but only in conjunction with a contemporaneous assignment of the lease. It is common for a seller to serve a notice and then sell that notice with the lease to a purchaser, who will take over the claim. There is no limit to the number of times that a tenant can exercise this right – so long as he is prepared to pay the costs for doing so.

Enfranchisement of Houses-Leasehold Reform Act 1967
What is the right?
The Leasehold Reform Act 1967 gives the tenant of a leasehold house who fulfils certain rules of qualification the right to acquire the freehold and any intermediate leases.

How do I qualify?
In looking at the rules of qualification under the 1967 Act, there are three basic questions that need to be answered. First, does the building qualify. Secondly, does the lease qualify. Thirdly, does the tenant qualify. In order for the building to qualify, it must be a 'house'. This has developed a wide definition and can mean a shop with a flat above, or a building converted to flats. However, one essential feature is that there must be no material over or under-hang with an adjoining building (if there is, then it is likely to be a flat).

The lease must comprise the whole of the house and it must be a long tenancy, i.e., a lease with an original term of more than 21 years. However, if it is a business tenancy, then it will not qualify if it is for an original term of 35 years or less.

The tenant must have owned the lease of the house for a period of at least two years before the date of the claim. Prior to the 2002 Act, it was also necessary for the tenant to occupy the house as his only or main residence for a three year period. The residence test has now been abolished save in limited circumstances.

If a house is mixed use so that there is a business tenancy (for example a building comprising a shop with a flat above) or if the house includes a flat which is subject to a qualifying lease under the 1993 Act (see above), then the tenant is still required to fulfil a residence test. However, it is modified so that the tenant has to occupy the house as his only or main residence only for two years or periods amounting in aggregate to two years in the preceding ten years.

Prior to the 2002 Act, the personal representatives of a deceased tenant had no right to make a claim., even where the deceased tenant was able to fulfill the qualifying conditions. However, such personal representatives can now make a claim provided that the right is exercised within a period of two years from the date of grant of probate.

The Price

The 1967 Act has three different valuation methods. In every case, the valuation date is the date of the claim.

If the house qualified pre-1933 (i.e. by not needing to rely on amendments made to the financial limits and/or low rent conditions by either the 1933 Act, the 1996 Act or the 2002 Act) and had a ratable value of less than £1,000 (£500 outside the

Greater London Area) on 31st March 1990 then the valuation is under section 9(1). This section expressly excludes any marriage value and restricts the value to a proportion of the site value.

If the house qualifies pre-1933 but did not have a ratable value of less than £1,000 (£500 outside the Greater London Area) on 31st March 1990, the valuation is under section 9 (1A). The valuation elements here are:

- The capitalised value of the landlords ground rent and the value of his reversion (being the present freehold vacant possession value deferred for the unexpired lease term; and
- 50% of the marriage value (the additional value released by the tenants ability to merge the freehold and leasehold interests) must be to the landlord although the marriage value will be deemed to be nil if the lease has an unexpired term of more than 80 years at the date of the claim.

If the house qualifies post-1933 (i.e. the claimant needs to rely on amendments made to the financial limits/low rent conditions by either the 1933 Act or the 2002 Act) then the valuation is under section 9 (1C). This is broadly the same as section 9(1A) valuation except that the freeholder can be compensated for loss in value of other property owned by him, including development value, consequent on the severance of the house from the other property.

How do I claim?

The procedure for a claim is relatively straightforward. The tenant serves his notice of claim, which is in prescribed form and needs to state (inter alia):

• a description of the house – but not necessarily with a plan;
• particulars to establish that the lease and tenant qualify;
• what the tenant thinks is the basis of valuation.

In addition to the price and the tenant's own legal costs and valuation fees, he will be required to reimburse the freeholder his legal costs and valuations fees.

The landlord is likely to respond with a procedural notice requiring payment of a deposit (equal to three times the rent payable under the lease) and asking the tenant to deduce title and (if a residence test is relevant) to produce evidence by statutory declaration that he fulfils the residence condition.

The landlord's valuer is also likely to inspect the house for the purpose of carrying out a valuation. The Act requires the landlord to state, within two months of the notice of claim being served, whether or not he admits the claim. If the claim is not admitted then the tenant must decide if he wishes to dispute the rejection through the courts. A freeholder cannot resist a claim on redevelopment grounds.

Disputes9(1C). This is broadly tame as a valuation

If the claim is admitted and either the terms of the conveyance or the price remain in dispute after two months following the date of the notice of claim, then either party can apply to the leasehold valuation tribunal for the matter in dispute to be determined. There are no time limits on the making of this application.

Completion

Once the terms of the conveyance and the purchase price have been agreed or determined by the leasehold valuation tribunal, the matter reverts to a conveyancing transaction with the parties proceeding to completion.

The tenant can withdraw at any time up to one month following the determination of the purchase price. Unlike collective enfranchisement and statutory lease extension claims, there are no strict procedural time limits. However, the tenant is liable for the landlord's costs as from the date of his notice of claim.

The extended lease option

The 1967 Act also allows the qualifying tenant of a house to take an extended lease of the house for a term of 50 years to expire after the term date of the existing lease at a modern ground rent throughout the extended term and without payment of a premium. This right has been little exercised in recent years not least because none of the amendments relating to the abolition of financial limits and the low rent test introduced by the 1993 Act, the 1996 Act and the 2002 Act apply to it. Furthermore, the extended lease originally had no statutory protection and carried no right to acquire the freehold.

However, following the 2002 Act, all tenancies extended under the 1967 Act now have security of tenure. Furthermore, the tenant under an extended lease now has the right to acquire the freehold, if he otherwise fulfils the qualifying conditions; in such cases, the purchase price will be determined in accordance with section 9(1C) but with modified assumptions.

Landlord and Tenant Act 1987: First Refusal

The Landlord and Tenant Act 1987 was chiefly concerned with enabling leaseholders to protect themselves against unreasonable service charges, and it made numerous amendments to tighten the rules originally laid down in the Landlord and Tenant Act 1985. In addition, it granted leaseholders the important right of first refusal if the freehold of their property is sold. It also allowed leaseholders to acquire the freehold if the property is being mismanaged: however, this right is little used because of the difficult procedures involved, and although it remains on the statute book it is likely to fall into complete disuse because the 2002 Act has now given leaseholders the same right without having to prove mismanagement.

The Right of First Refusal (RFR) is provided by Part 1 of the Landlord and Tenant Act 1987 (the 1987 Act) as amended by the Housing Act 1996.

Where a landlord is proposing to sell his interest in a building containing flats in relation to which the RFR exists, he must, by law, first offer it to the tenants before offering it on the open market. He must serve formal notices on the tenants telling them what he is intending and must provide time for them to consider the offer; he cannot sell to another party during that time, nor offer the interest to anyone else at a price less than that proposed to the tenants or on different terms. Breach of these legal obligations by the landlord is a criminal offence. If the landlord sells without providing the Right of First Refusal, the tenants can serve a notice on the new owner demanding details of the transaction, including the price paid; they can then take action to force the new owner to sell to them at the price he paid.

It is important to understand certain key principles of the RFR:

- it is not a means of forcing a landlord to sell his freehold interest in a property (this is provided by the enfranchisement provisions of the Leasehold Reform, Housing and Urban Development Act 1993). It is an opportunity for the tenants to purchase that interest before it is offered on the open market or by auction.

- the right follows a landlord's decision to sell and the tenants can only react to the landlord's offer. He can withdraw the offer at any time before the contract is binding.

- the right is available both to leaseholders and regulated (fair rent) tenants but not to houses occupied as single dwellings.

- the price is set by the landlord, or by auction where the landlord decides to sell that way. There is no right for that price to be determined by a Leasehold Valuation Tribunal or anyone else. However the landlord cannot sell or offer the interest to another party on different terms or at a lower price than that originally offered within 12 months of his notice, unless he again offers the Right to the existing tenants on the new terms and/or at the lower figure.

- the price set may, in some circumstances, be lower than that which could be achieved through a collective enfranchisement. However, it could also be higher.

- the requirement to make the offer and the procedure involved is set out in the Act. If a landlord fails to comply with any of these statutory requirements he commits a criminal offence. The requirements also apply where the landlord's interest is being sold by a Receiver, a Trustee in or an Executor following grant of probate.

- the right is not available to tenants of local authorities, housing associations, nor, in some cases, where the landlord lives in the building.

Buildings, landlords and qualifying tenants

For the RFR to exist, the building, the landlord and the tenants have to meet certain requirements.

The building

There are three requirements for the building to be subject to the RFR:

- it must contain at least two flats; and
- No more than 50% of the building to be in non-residential use; and
- more than 50% of the flats in the building must be held by 'qualifying tenants'.

The legislation does not define what is intended as a building, but it is generally understood to mean a separate building or, in some cases, a part of a building which may be divided vertically from another part.

In the absence of a legal definition, a common sense approach should apply as to what normally constitutes a building and whether it is capable of development without substantially affecting the rest of the building. So, floors of flats above a shop are not a separate building but one half of a pair of semi-detached houses converted into flats is a separate building from its neighbour.

There must be at least two flats in the building, so the right does not apply to houses occupied as one unit - but will, of course, apply to a house which has been converted into flats.

The building will be excluded from the RFR if more than 50% (excluding the common areas) is not in residential use, say offices or shops. The measurement excludes any common parts of the residential building, such as staircases, landings etc. The

Act refers to parts of the premises occupied or intended to be occupied for non-residential purposes. A building could be excluded if it contained empty spaces which made up more than half the building which the landlord intended to use for non-residential purposes, such as storage.

The landlord

The RFR does not apply to the following landlords:

- most housing authorities (local Councils, New Towns and Development Corporations);
- registered social landlords and fully mutual housing associations which are not registered;
- charitable housing trusts; and resident landlords who live in the building where the following two conditions apply:
- the building is not a purpose-built block of flats, that is, it must be a property, a house for example, which has been converted into flats since its original construction; and
- the landlord genuinely lives in the building as his only or principal residence and has done so for more than 12 months.

Immediate landlord

The RFR only applies when the immediate landlord of the tenants decides to sell. The immediate landlord is the one to whom the rent or ground rent is paid and who will be entitled to vacant possession of the flat when the lease expires. Where a landlord has a lease for less than seven years (or longer, but which is terminable within the first seven years) his landlord is also subject to the RFR in relation to those premises.

Qualifying tenants

The RFR is restricted to qualifying tenants.
These include leaseholders and most fixed or periodic tenancies, but specifically excludes shorthold or assured tenancies, business and agricultural tenancies, tenancies which are dependant upon employment (and any sub-tenants of any of these).

Someone who is a tenant of three or more flats in the building (as leaseholder or tenant) will not be a qualifying tenant of any of the flats and will not be entitled to the Right of First Refusal.

The Procedure under the 1987 Act for the right of first refusal is as follows.

- The freeholder notifies all qualifying tenants of his desire to sell and of the price at which he is willing to do so (including any non-monetary element). The notice must state the proposed method of sale: for instance, by conveyance or by auction.

- The freeholder must give the qualifying tenants at least two months to respond; and, if they say they wish to buy, at least a further two months (28 days if the sale is to be by auction) to come up with a nominee purchaser to acquire the freehold on their behalf. This could conceivably be in an individual or an organisation that already exists, but is much more likely to be a company set up specially for the purpose by the qualifying tenants, and under their control.

- During this period, the landlord and the qualifying tenants may wish to take the opportunity to negotiate the price.

- If a majority of the qualifying tenants have put forward a nominee purchaser and agreed with the freeholder on a price, the freeholder may not sell to anyone else.

- If the qualifying tenants fail to put forward a nominee purchaser, or if a mutually acceptable price is not agreed, the freeholder has twelve months to sell to someone else in accordance with the original notice (by auction, if that was the method specified; and in any other case for a price not less than that originally offered to the qualifying tenants). If no sale has taken place within twelve months, the freeholder must start the procedure again from scratch if he wishes to sell.

5

FORMING AND MANAGING A FLAT MANAGEMENT COMPANY

Chapter 5

The Formation of a Flat Management Company

Flat owners, although individuals in their own right, are joined in the need to ensure that the management of their flats and common areas is carried out cost effectively and efficiently. So far, in this book we have concentrated on the rights and obligations of leaseholders and freeholders. However, if leaseholders wish to exercise the right to enfranchise, as described in the previous chapter, or to simply purchase the freehold on offer from the landlord, then a vehicle for the ownership of the freehold and the management of the flats, will need to be created.

Each flat owner will want to ensure that a proper structure is in place for management and for enforcing obligations between flat owners and for how the building as a whole is maintained and ensured.

What is the purpose of a company set up to manage flats?

At the beginning of the book, the nature of a lease was outlined. Under the terms of flat leases, the flat owner will have entered into covenants which are inserted in the lease and are necessary for the efficient running of the block. Without some separate body enforcing the covenants, management of the building would break down. The block would soon fall into disrepair, the common areas remain unclean and untended and the overall appearance of the block would diminish, along with the value of the properties.

Although there are a number of ways of managing a block of flats, or a house split into flats, such as an individual ownership of the freehold, it is the flat management company which is the recommended vehicle for management of the freehold, after enfranchisement or a straight purchase of the freehold. For the rest of this chapter we will discuss the setting up of such a company and how to go about administering it.

The management company

The company set up to own the freehold and to manage the leases and provide services will be a limited liability company. A limited company is a distinct entity having a separate legal capacity from its shareholders, or members. The company's members have control of the company which they exercise through voting rights. The company may be limited by shares or by guarantee.

A limited company is defined by the concept of limited liability which means that the liability of the members to contribute to the debts of the company is limited. They will have either purchased shares in the company or guaranteed to contribute a fixed sum to the company.

In many cases, a proportion of flat owners in a block will not be interested in participating as members of a company, even though they own a share. Ultimate success of a flat management company will, usually, depend on the will and drive of a few members. Without this drive then the company will not come into being and effective management will not be delivered.

If enough members are enthusiastic then a committee will need to be formed with delegated powers to be able to go forward and set up the limited company. A solicitor will need to be appointed to incorporate the company and to transfer ownership of the freehold from the freeholder to the management company. There will be a number of supporting requirements for the company such as:

- Banking facilities- the committee will need to arrange for a current account to be set up with a local bank, agree signatories to the account and provide the signed mandate for the bank. The bank will offer you further advice;
- Accountants will need to be appointed. This will certainly be the case where there is a lot of money flowing through the company and VAT is involved. If the cash flow is minimal then it may be the case that simple accounts are kept by the members of the committee, by someone with the requisite skills. However, this is a function that will need to be decided as soon as possible.
- The registered office will need to be decided upon.

Other areas of administration may be printed letterheads. Again, some thought should be given as to whether this is really necessary.

A company will have Memoranda and Articles of association. The memoranda and articles of association regulate the activities of the company and define what it can and cannot do. Flat management companies will usually have specific provisions in the articles, limiting membership of the company to those who own a flat in the block or house. Forms of articles used by flat management companies are normally created by the solicitors appointed to set up the company. Although there are model articles on companies house website these are not generally applicable to flat management companies.

Transferring ownership of the freehold to the new company

The solicitor acting on behalf of the flat owners in the conveyance of the freehold will have a duty to determine good title to the building. All aspects of the ownership of the building and any future matters that may affect ownership will be checked. Many of the tasks undertaken by a solicitor will be the same as if a property was being purchased in the normal way. Local authority searches will be undertaken and questions asked relating to any outstanding debts. The lease will be examined, with a particular emphasis on the provisions for payment of service charges and ground rent, when and how these should be paid and the financial year relating to the company. Of importance here is the question of conveyance of the freehold whilst there are outstanding arrears. Does the newly formed management company wish to undertake responsibility for outstanding arrears or will it insist that these are paid up before transfer? This is an important point and it is good practice to ensure that all arrears are paid up so that the company and its members are starting from a clean slate.

Appointment of officers

It is more than likely that all flat owners will be shareholders of the management company. As with all companies, shareholders will delegate the running of the company to appointed officers. This is necessary as otherwise the whole operation can lose focus and also disagreements can set in.

Companies have a minimum legal requirement on formation-there must be at least two officers at formation, a Director and a Company secretary. There need only be one director in office at any one time.

The role of the company secretary is of particular importance as this person has the most work to do in administering the company, giving notice to the members of meetings, preparing notices, drafting resolutions, preparing minutes and filing all statutory forms. The latter task is important because failure to file accounts and annual returns to companies house results in an automatic fine, currently one hundred pounds.

The full details of company's house, the address and supporting information will be given on incorporation of the company. Most flat management companies, following incorporation, are best managed by a small committee of flat owners, with officers appointed to carry out specific tasks. This committee can rotate on a periodic basis, if needs be.

Common administrative requirements of a flat management company are as follows:

- Insurance
- Maintenance and repairs
- Banking
- Rent and service charge collection
- Preparation of annual budget estimates
- Maintenance of books and accounts
- Annual audit and annual accounts
- Security of property
- Keeping flat owners informed as to the management

It is also very important that all members of the flat management company have read and understood the lease as the lease will define the scope of landlord and leaseholder obligations. For example, repairing obligations are clearly outlined in leases and the policy of the landlord, and the ultimate strategy concerning repairs will need to be defined by the contents of the lease. Some leases will state that a landlord is responsible for all repairs to the structure and exterior of the property, including window frames and front doors. Other leases will limit that responsibility to the structure and exterior, excluding window frames. Ultimately, the policies and practice adopted by the management company will affect how much money is spent and by whom. To repeat, all policy of the management company must be formulated in accordance with the requirements of the lease and this must be clearly communicated to residents.

Insurance considerations

Insurance is normally collected through a service charge. The lease will, in nearly all cases, impose an insurance obligation on the landlord. The insurance will cover the main structure of the building and also public liability. As we have seen, leaseholders have the right to question insurance premiums. However, one advantage of being a shareholder in a company that owns the freehold is that you have complete control of the costs of insurance.

All leaseholders must be aware of the insurance policy, what it covers and how to claim in the event of an insurable loss. Likewise, the officer delegated to look after insurance must be fully acquainted with the nature of the policy and must be prepared to renegotiate the policy every year, ensuring value for money and the best possible cover.

Maintenance and repairs.

The management company, through the freeholders obligations in the lease, will have responsibility for the structure and exterior of the block. As we have seen, this will be more specifically defined in the lease. The management company will be responsible for the foundations of the block, external walls, roof and other supporting structures. In addition, any lifts or other machinery will be the responsibility of the company along with the general maintenance of the common parts. This will include boundary fences and drainage external to flats.

This particular task, and planning for future payments is onerous. The director dealing with maintenance will need to take on board the following points:

- A full assessment of the company's liabilities for repair and maintenance will need to be undertaken through an analysis of the lease. This will need to be summarised and communicated to all leaseholders
- Quotations for work will need to be obtained before works are carried out. The director dealing with this will need to be fully acquainted with the provisions of Landlord and Tenant Acts as outlined earlier in this book. This is of fundamental importance. Remember, any money spent over a certain amount cannot be recovered unless the law has been adhered to. The important exception is emergencies.

The anticipation of future expenditure is very important in respect of future requirements. A decision has to be made as to whether leaseholders are charged as and when works are needed or whether a monthly "sinking fund" is levied, through the service charge, in order to cater for any future expenditure.

Remember that any money raised must be placed on an interest bearing account and placed in trust. Your bank can advise you on this aspect. The main point is to have some idea of requirements over the long term, say 25 years and to work out how much money will be needed to cater for this.

This method of planning is infinitely more preferable to charging as and when repairs are needed, as money may not be available at this point and management problems may occur. Money paid into a sinking fund is not recoverable by individual leaseholders on sale as this payment is for wear and tear and belongs to the company.

Banking

Money needs to be collected from flat owners, either by standing order or direct debit and receipts issued. The director responsible for banking will usually hold the mandate for cheque signing, along with at least one other person. Authorisation for signing cheques should never be vested in one person as this can lead to misappropriation of funds. The person dealing with banking will probably also be the person dealing with the overall treasury side of the business, including accounts and bookkeeping.

Rent and Service charge collection

This is usually delegated to one person. Without doubt, the best way to collect service charges and ground rent is through direct debit on a periodic basis, usually monthly. A healthy cash balance is always necessary in order to meet bills.

Preparation of annual budgets

Each year, an assessment of the likely expenditure for the forthcoming financial year will need to be undertaken. This will mean scrutinising the expenditure to date and assessing next year's expenditure on the basis of this. Where very heavy costs are anticipated, usually on an item of major repair, all leaseholders will need to be informed. As described above, if there is money in the pot to deal with it, life becomes that much easier than if all flat owners are to be billed.

One important point: short term thinking, resulting in short term savings for leaseholders is the very worst way of managing the economic process relating to property management. A monthly major repairs charge, through the service charge is, in the view of the author, absolutely necessary.

When it is prepared, the budget must be given to all leaseholders (whether members of the company or not) and a clear month should be allowed for any feedback. In reality, with everyone so close to the process, then agreement can be reached before this time. When the budget has been accepted then a copy will need to be sent to all leaseholders, as the final copy and instructions given concerning the changing of direct debits.

If the management company is in the position of having no money to hand to carry out works and the billing of individual leaseholders is necessary then particular care should be taken to ensure that people are in receipt of clear advice concerning the amount for the work, their contribution, when it needs to be paid and how they can raise the money needed. It could be that advice needs to be given about loans, arrangements can be made to spread the payments over several years and so on. It really depends on the situation of the management company concerned. Again, if you can avoid getting into this position through prudent management of charges, then life will be that much easier. A model service charge budget and accounts are shown at the end of the chapter.

Maintenance of accounting records

This function will be performed (preferably) by the same director who deals with other financial matters. In addition, the supervision of the preparation of annual accounts will be undertaken by the same person.

Security of property

This will normally be the responsibility of the person responsible for maintenance and repairs. Security will vary depending on the size and nature of the block of flats in question.

Keeping flat owners informed

Without doubt, one of the major problems in all organisations is that of communication, keeping others informed. If this can be achieved successfully then management becomes that much easier. One person will usually be appointed to do this.

Directors meetings

Directors of flat management companies should aim to have at least two formal meetings a year to review the operations of the company. Of course, meetings will be held informally at different times to discuss various issues. These should always be minuted. However, the six monthly meetings constitute formal meetings of directors. The company secretary will attend such meetings and will minute the proceedings and the minutes of the last meeting will need to be approved and signed as an accurate record. Some decisions may require a vote, which can be the majority of those present, with the chair holding a casting vote in cases of deadlock. The chairman is usually appointed by the board to oversee the proceedings of the meetings.

Shareholders meetings

Meetings of the shareholders or members are known as general meetings. General meetings of a company is where the formal business of the company is conducted. All members of the company are entitled to attend and they are empowered to vote on certain matters. There are two types of meeting, the annual general meeting and the extraordinary general meeting.

The annual general meeting is where the directors of a company will subject themselves to the scrutiny of its members. It is necessary, by law, for a company to hold an AGM once every calendar year. The first AGM of a newly incorporated company will not be held until 18 months after incorporation.

Each subsequent AGM must happen not more than 15 months after the last one. Details concerning the nature, frequency and type of meeting can be obtained from companies house.

The company secretary will call the AGM, the notice stating the following:

- A statement that the meeting is an AGM
- Details of the meeting, date, time and place
- An agenda of the business to be dealt with
- Details of the rights of members to appoint proxies to vote

This notice is served on all directors, members and auditors of the company. 21 days clear notice must be given of the AGM. If accounts are being presented at the meeting then copies have to be circulated with the notice.

The usual business of an AGM is as follows:

- Election of officers
- Presentation of accounts
- Appointment of auditors
- Directors reports

Any other business should be allowed for at the end. Certain people may have grievances and it is good practice to allow these to be aired.

The articles of association will provide details of a necessary quorum in order to enable the meeting to proceed and decisions to be taken. Minutes must be kept and an annual return, which will normally be sent to the company will need to be submitted to companies house along with the accounts.

The meeting of members other than the AGM is known as an extraordinary general meeting. This is hardly ever necessary. However, the facility for such a meeting does exist. The extraordinary general meeting would only be called in rare circumstances, such as the need to change an aspect of the running of the company which needs urgent agreement, this being the winding up of the company, a serious financial crisis and so on.

The company secretary will send a notice to members and can dispense with the notice period if necessary. The business at the EGM is transacted by the shareholders voting on whichever resolutions are proposed.

Model service charge budget

ESTIMATE OF SERVICE CHARGES-VICTORIA HOUSE, ALBERT ROAD, WALLINFORD. PERIOD 2013/2014

This estimate of charges has been prepared in accordance with the Landlord And Tenant Acts 1985 and 1987.

Period 5th April 2013 to 31st March 2014.

Charges	Current year charges
Charges 2011/2012	
Cleaning of common parts	
Gardening	
Electricity	
Gas	
Insurance	
Day to day maintenance	
Major repairs fund	
Cyclical maintenance (Painting and decorating at three yearly intervals)	
Total	Total

Number of flats

Charge per unit   Per annum

                 Per month

Your landlord is (Registered company)

Notes to above budget. It may be necessary to attach further notes with the budget for information purposes.

Model service charge accounts

(Registered company)

Expenditure statement for 5th April 2013 to 31st March 2014

Victoria House, Albert Road, Wallinford.

Service charge expenditure:

Cleaning of common parts

Gardening

Electricity

Gas

Insurance

Day to day maintenance

Major repairs fund

Cyclical maintenance

Total expenditure

Proportion payable in respect of

Less money paid on account

Balance due

Add ground rent for coming year
Any other

Note that this is a simple form of accounts for example only. It is highly likely that an accountant will prepare a form of accounts for leaseholders.

GLOSSARY OF TERMS

Assignment The transfer of a lease or tenancy from one person to another, usually by sale.

Blanket condition A term in a lease or tenancy that, if taken literally, would impose unreasonable constraints on the use of the premises.

Conveyance The transfer of a freehold from one person to another, usually by sale.

Determination A lease or tenancy is said to be determined when it is brought to an end by a positive act by either the landlord (freeholder) or tenant (leaseholder), as opposed to coming to an end because its term has expired. An outstanding example of a word used in one way by lawyers and another by everyone else.

Enfranchisement (individual) A lease is enfranchised when the leaseholder acquires the freehold. This has the effect of ending the lease and leaving the former leaseholder in sole possession of the freehold.

Enfranchisement (collective) The acquisition of the freehold on behalf of a number of leaseholders acting together.

Exclusive possession The right of a leaseholder or tenant to exclude other people, especially the landlord or freeholder, from the property.

Extension A lease is said to be extended when a longer term is agreed by both parties or (more usually) when it is replaced by a fresh lease with longer to run. The latter can happen either by agreement or as a result of the leaseholder exercising legal rights.

Fixed term A fixed term tenancy or lease is one with a defined ending date, as opposed to a periodic tenancy.

Forfeiture The ultimate penalty if the leaseholder has breached the terms of the lease: the courts can end it and return the property to the freeholder.

Freeholder The owner of the strongest title to land available under English law. Freehold is tantamount to outright ownership and is treated as such in this book. The term 'freeholder' is used throughout to refer to the person granting the lease, although this will not always be the case in practice in practice - see the section on *Head leases and subleases* in Chapter One.

Ground Rent A usually notional payment required under a lease, a source of income to the freeholder and a reminder to the leaseholder that he does not own the property outright.

Head lease When a leaseholder grants one or more subleases, the original lease is called the head lease.

Landlord The granter of a lease, tenancy, or licence.

Lease Strictly, the terms lease and tenancy are interchangeable. In this book, a lease is a tenancy with a fixed term of over seven years.

Leaseholder In this book, a tenant for a fixed term exceeding seven years.

Leasehold valuation tribunal A special committee appointed to settle disputes between freeholders and leaseholders arising from the enfranchisement or extension of leases under the 1967, 1987, and 1993 Acts.

Licence Permission to occupy land not amounting to a tenancy or lease, usually because exclusive possession is not granted.

Long lease Defined for various purposes under the 1967, 1987, and 1993 Acts as a lease originally granted for a fixed term of over 21 years.

Low rent A level of rent defined in the 1967, 1987, and 1993 Acts in ways that are intended to exclude the rent likely to be paid under a periodic tenancy or short fixed term tenancy.

Managing agent An organisation or (seldom) individual appointed by a freeholder to carry out some or all of his management responsibilities.

Management agreement Legal contract appointing a managing agent.

Management fee Payment due from the freeholder to the managing agent.

Marriage value Value by which the elements brought together by a lease enfranchisement, or extension, exceed their combined value as separate entities before it took place. The marriage value is sometimes a component in calculating the premium when leases are extended or enfranchised.

Mixed tenure A mixed tenure block is one that contains both leasehold and tenanted property.

Mortgagee The person or (usually) financial institution lending money against the security of property. Not to be confused with the following.

Mortgagor The owner of property, using it as security to raise a loan. 'Mortgagee' and 'mortgagor' are often confused, but if it is remembered that the owner of the property can be said to have mortgaged it, the difference becomes clear.

Nominee purchaser Whoever is chosen by the leaseholders involved in collective enfranchisement to be the new owner of the freehold: usually a company they have set up for the purpose.

Onerous condition A term in a lease or tenancy that seriously affects its market value.

Open market value The value of any saleable item assuming a willing seller and a willing buyer. The open market value of a freehold or a lease is a component in calculating the premium when leases are extended or enfranchised.

Peppercorn A notional rent is often called a peppercorn - an unusually fanciful piece of legal jargon..

Period of grace Leases sold under the right to buy, and occasionally other leases, contain an estimate of future service charges, usually for the first five years of the lease. During this 'period of grace' any spending above the estimate cannot be recovered.

Periodic A periodic tenancy is one that runs from period to period (usually week to week or month to month) until something intervenes to stop it.

Pre-charging Charging for services in advance: used to build up a sinking fund.

Premium The payment due by the leaseholder to the freeholder when a lease is enfranchised or extended.

Qualifying leaseholders (or qualifying tenants) The tenants or leaseholders that qualify for the various rights, under the 1967, 1987, or 1993 Acts, to enfranchise or extend leases. The qualifications vary depending which right is being exercised under which Act.

Quiet enjoyment The right of leaseholders and tenants not to have their use of the property interfered with by the landlord: closely allied to exclusive possession.

Recognised tenants' association Body of leaseholders and/or tenants recognised by the freeholder for consultation purposes.

Re-entry Regaining possession of a property, for instance at the end of a tenancy or lease.

Rent Payment of (almost always) money in exchange for being allowed to occupy property under a lease, tenancy, or licence.

Residence test Requirement for most purposes under the 1967, 1987, and 1993 Acts that a leaseholder must live on the premises, or have done so in the recent past. The exact test varies depending which right is being exercised.

Reversioner The person to whom possession will revert when the existing lease or tenancy comes to an end; usually the freeholder.

Right to buy A scheme, originally under the Housing Act 1980, allowing tenants of local authorities and some housing associations to buy their homes at a substantial discount.

Service charge Payment by leaseholders and tenants for services provided by the freeholder.

Shared ownership A scheme for assisted house purchase on part-buy, part-rent terms.

Sinking fund A fund built up on the service charge account by pre-charging.

Staircasing The purchase by a shared owner of an additional share of the property.

Sublease A lease granted by a leaseholder.

Tenant For the purpose of this book, someone holding a periodic tenancy or a tenancy granted for a fixed term of less than seven years.

Term The time for which a lease or fixed term tenancy will run.

Index

Appendix 1

A Summary of the 2002 Commonhold and Leasehold Reform Act

The Commonhold and Leasehold Reform Act became law in May 2002, and was implemented in stages. Part 1 of the Act introduced a new form of tenure called commonhold. Commonhold is applicable to new developments but is not compulsory. Existing blocks of flats can also convert to commonhold voluntarily if all leaseholders agree. Commonhold essentially means that a company (commonhold association), with each commonholder having a share, is formed. Individual flats are freehold and the common parts are owned and managed collectively. A commonhold association will have a commonhold community statement which is a statement defining how the commonhold will be managed.

The Act provides details about commonhold and the management of commonhold flats. These cover accounting and budgeting and also details about commonhold associations plus other elements. of the Act and introduces a new no-fault right to manage, which will enable leaseholders to take over the management of their building without having to prove fault on the part of the landlord or pay him or her any compensation. Enfranchisement (collective purchase of the freehold) is made easier for leaseholders of flats and houses. Lease extensions are easier to obtain. Leaseholders of houses who previously extended their leases can now buy the freehold. The rights of those who have inherited a leasehold house are improved, leaseholders rights against unreasonable service charges are strengthened, and accounting rules are strengthened. In addition, lease variations are easier to obtain, the right to seek appointment of a new manager is strengthened, landlords must now demand ground rent in writing before they can collect and the roles of Leasehold Valuation Tribunals are consolidated and strengthened.

The Right to Manage

Although long leaseholders of flats have purchased the right to live in their property, control of the management, maintenance and insurance of the property normally remains in the hands of the landlord. Leaseholders are normally obliged under their leases to meet the full costs of the landlords functions, but enjoy little control over the quality and value for money of these services.

In order to counter this, the Act introduced the 'no fault' right to manage.

The Act provides that:

- leaseholders will be able to collectively take over the management duties for the building, for example leaseholders will be able to have a greater degree of control over the level and cost of services and appoint their own choice of managing agents and select their own insurers
- leaseholders will not have to prove any fault or shortcomings on the part of the landlord in order to exercise the right
- leaseholders will not be required to pay any compensation to the landlord for exercising the right.

Qualifying requirements

The eligibility requirements will ensure that neither a minority of qualifying tenants, nor a minority of the residents in a block, could take control. The eligibility requirements are as follows:

- Leaseholders must own a long lease (more than 21 years)
- Where the lease is a shared ownership lease, the leaseholder

would have to hold a 100% share of the equity

- Leaseholders must become members of a company which is properly constituted for the purposes of collective management – that will be a private company limited by guarantee (see chapter six) which must include the exercise of the right to manage as one of its main objects.

- At least two thirds of the flats in the building would have to be held by long leaseholders, and the participating leaseholders would have to hold the leases of at least half of the flats in the blocks.

- RTM will apply to any premises containing two or more flats held by qualifying tenants. This includes both a self-contained building and a vertically separated part of the building (for example a converted terraced house)

- Premises would also include any associated parts, such as garages and gardens, which are for the sole use of the residents of the block in question.

Exclusions-The following are excluded from the RTM:

- Properties in mixed residential and non-residential use where the internal floor are of the non-residential parts exceeds 25% of the total internal floor area of the property.

- Any premises which have been converted into flats (or a mixture of flats and other units used as dwellings e.g. bedsits) if the converted building contains no more than four units and the landlord (or an adult member of the family) lives in one of these units and has done so for the previous twelve months.

- Any premises where the landlord is a local authority. Local authority tenants already have a separate right to manage.

- Where an RTM management body loses the management of a

property for any reason. In such circumstances the block in question will be excluded from any exercise of RTM for four years from the date that the body ceased their management duties, unless the permission of a Leasehold Valuation Tribunal is obtained.

Almost certainly, if leaseholders chose to go down this road, then the appointment of a Chartered Surveyor or Lawyer would be necessary to guide the process through.

Lease renewals for flats
The right for leaseholders to acquire a new lease for their property, which adds on 90 years over and above the existing term, is an individual right arising out of the 1993 Leasehold, Housing and Urban Development Act. The existing regime is modified as follows:

- Removal of the low rent test
- Abolition of the residence test, which will benefit leaseholders who occupy their flat as a second home or sub-let it. However, a tenant must have been a leaseholder for two years prior to the application to extend the lease
- Provides that any marriage value (increase in value by extending) be shared equally between landlord and leaseholder; and to presume that there is no marriage value where the lease runs for over 80 years.
- Helps representatives of deceased leaseholders by allowing them to qualify for the right where the deceased qualified immediately before they died. The right would be exercisable for a period of six months starting from the date of the grant of probate or letters of administration.

Enfranchisement

The new Act includes a number of changes to the collective enfranchisement provisions in Chapter 1 of Part 1 of the Leasehold Reform, Housing and Urban Development Act 1993.

Rules under the 1993 Act
- To be eligible leaseholders must be qualifying tenants, which means that leaseholders must hold a lease which when originally granted was for a period of more than 21 years. This does not include a business lease.
- The lease must also be at a low rent-there is a complex test for this, unless it is for a particularly low term (over 35 years).
- The building must include at least two flats occupied by qualifying tenants. At least two thirds of all the flats in the building must be occupied by qualifying tenants.
- Any non-domestic component in the block must not exceed 10% of the floor area.
- The building does not qualify if it is a converted property of four or fewer flats and a resident landlord or a member of their family is living in one of them
- The group of qualifying tenants seeking to enfranchise must include at least two thirds of all the qualifying tenants in the block
- At least half the residents must satisfy the residence test, that is, they must have occupied the flat for the last 12 months or for periods adding up to three out of the last ten years.

Revised eligibility criteria in the 2002 Act
- Abolition of the residence test
- For individual leaseholders the low rent test is be abolished

- The resident landlord exemption would be restricted to cases where the resident landlord had carried out the conversion
- The requirement to include at least two thirds of the qualifying tenants in the block is removed but the group would continue to have to hold the leases of at least half of the flats in the block
- The threshold for the non domestic component is raised to 25%
- Participating leaseholders must be members of a company which is properly constituted for the purposes of ownership and management
- All qualifying leaseholders have the right to participate in the enfranchisement process by becoming members of the company.

Valuation

The 1993 Act sets down certain valuation rules and principles which must be followed in calculating the price payable for the freehold. In outline, the price payable is an aggregate of three components:

- the open market value of the freeholders interest in the premises
- The freeholders share of the 'marriage value'
- Any compensation for losses.

The freeholder is also entitled to recover his or her reasonable costs of dealing with the enfranchisement, other than the costs associated with appearing before a LVT.

Revised changes to valuation

The 2002 Act introduced the following measures:

- to share the marriage value equally between landlord and leaseholder
- to presume that there is no marriage value where the leases of all participating leaseholders have more than 80 years to run
- to remove the unfettered right of appeal to the Lands Tribunal against leasehold valuation (LVT) decisions, so that permission would need to be sought from the LVT or Lands Tribunal.

Service charges and administration charges

The 2002 Act introduced a number of changes to leaseholders rights in relation to service charges under the Landlord and Tenant Act 1985. Rights generally are:

- the right to be consulted about major works
- the right for service charges to be reasonable
- the right to challenge the reasonableness of any service charge or of the standard of work
- the right to certain information about service charges

The 2002 Act:
- Requires landlords to provide annual accounting statements that provide information about monies paid into a service charge fund, or standing to the credit of the service charge fund as well as costs incurred by the landlord. Leaseholders will be able to withhold service charges if this requirement has not been met

- requires landlords to provide leaseholders with a summary of their rights and obligations in relation to service charges
- gives leaseholders the right to inspect documentatluu relevant to their accounting statements within 21 days of their request. Leaseholders will also be able to take copies of that information, or have copies provided to them on payment of a reasonable fee
- clarifies that leaseholders can challenge service charges at a Leasehold Valuation Tribunal where the amount has already been paid to a landlord
- requires landlords to hold service charges funds in a designated separate client account. Leaseholders will have the right to ask for proof that this requirement has been met
- provides that where leaseholders have reasonable grounds for believing that the landlord is not holding their service charges in a separate account they will be able to withhold service charges
- provides that it will be a criminal offence to fail without reasonable excuse to use separate client accounts
- provides that service charges are held in trust, even where only one leaseholder has to pay them
- enables leaseholders to inspect the insurance policy for the insurance for their building, without having first to ask for a summary of the cover. Leaseholders can take copies or have copies provided to them for a reasonable fee
- extends the existing definition of service charges to cover improvements, and allow it to be further extended by regulations
- gives leaseholders a new right to challenge unreasonable

administration charges payable under the lease

- simplifies and strengthen the existing right of leaseholders to be consulted about major works. The requirement to consult leaseholders about major works would apply when the amount payable by any leaseholder exceeds a prescribed sum

- introduces a new requirement for landlords to consult before entering into contracts for the provision of ongoing works or services lasting for longer than 12 months. Disputes over compliance with the requirements would be transferred from the courts to the Leasehold valuation Tribunals.

Leasehold Houses

The Act introduced a number of changes to the rights for leaseholders of houses. The new rights, which amend the 1967 Leasehold reform Act, are as follows:

- The residence test is replaced with a new requirement that the leaseholder must have held the lease for at least two years.
- The low rent test is abolished.
- Leaseholders can buy the freehold of their property once the lease is extended.
- Where marriage value is payable, it will be split 50%-50% between leaseholder and landlord.
- Marriage value is disregarded where the lease has over 80 years left to run.
- The rights of those who inherit a leasehold house are improved.
- Where leaseholders extend the lease but do not buy the freehold they will become entitled to an assured tenancy under part 1 of the Housing Act 1988 when their extended lease expires.

- The Act includes sub-tenants who would not otherwise qualify.

Absent landlords

The Act also simplified the procedures for enfranchisement of houses where the landlord cannot be traced. Leaseholders can apply to a county court (rather than the High Court) for a vesting order.

Leasehold Valuation Tribunals will determine the price payable rather than a surveyor appointed by the Lands Tribunal as is the current procedure.

Ground rent and forfeiture

Most long residential leases require an annual ground rent to be paid. The 2002 Act provides:

- that a leaseholder should only be liable for any ground rent payable under the lease if a written demand has been received from the landlord.
- That the landlord would be prohibited by law from making any additional charge in respect of the rent if the rent is paid within 30 days.
- That the landlord would also be prevented from starting forfeiture action for non-payment of ground rent unless a demand has been made. And at least 30 days have elapsed since the demand.

Forfeiture

The 2002 Act:

- Introduced new restrictions on the commencement of forfeiture proceedings, including the service of notices under section 146 of the Law of Property Act 1925. Landlords can only take action for forfeiture when a court or LVT has determined that a breach of covenant or condition of the lease has occurred. This provision addressed the problem of landlords who threaten forfeiture proceedings on spurious grounds in order to persuade leaseholders to pay unreasonable charges.

Leasehold Valuation Tribunals
Leasehold Valuation Tribunals currently deal with a wide range of disputes involving residential leasehold property. For example they deal with disputes over valuation for purposes of enfranchisement and lease renewal. In addition, they deal with service charge disputes. The new Act introduced changes to the LVT's designed to make them more effective.

The 2002 Act:
- consolidated the law on the LVT's procedure and constitution
- extended the LVT's jurisdiction to be able to make a determination as to the liability of leaseholders to pay the service charge.
- Allowed landlords to apply to the LVT, before carrying out specific works, for a determination that the costs of the specific works fall to be paid by way of service charges under the relevant leases.
- Allowed the LVT to make determinations as to the liability to pay an administration charge.
- Granted the LVT's powers to enforce directions.
- Granted the LVT power to award costs where, in the opinion of the tribunal, a party has in bringing or conducting proceedings before the Tribunal acted frivolously, vexatiously, abusively, disruptively or otherwise unreasonably.

- Provided that all appeals to the Lands Tribunal from the LVT be subject to permission of the LVT concerned or the Lands Tribunal.
- Provided that where both parties agree disputes can be dealt with by way of written representation.

Variation of leases and appointment of a manager

Leaseholders enjoy rights under part 1V of the Landlord and Tenant Act 1987 to seek variations to their leases. The 2002 Act introduced measures to improve the operation of these rights. In relation to lease variation, Act:

- transferred jurisdiction for applications to vary leases from county courts to Leasehold Valuation Tribunals
- clarified and extend the grounds for applying for a variation of a lease, such as leases that did not provide for a building to be insured under a single policy
- provided a right for any party to a lease of a dwelling to apply to an LVT for an order varying the provisions of a lease on the grounds that a fixed administration charge specified in the lease, or a formula for determining such a charge, was unreasonable.

Leaseholders currently enjoy rights to seek the appointment of a new manager under Part 2 of the 1987 Act. The 2002 Act contained measures to improve the operation of that right.

Amendments to the appointment for a Manager Regime

Amendments will:

- make clear that leaseholders can apply to a LVT for the appointment of a new manager where a lease provides for management functions to be carried out by a third party manager rather than the landlord

- provide that failure to hold service charge funds in trust or in a separate client account will be a specific ground on which to seek the appointment of a new manager
- restrict the current exemption for resident landlords in converted houses. The exemption would in future not apply if at least half of the flats in the building are held on long leases which are not business tenancies under part 2 of the Landlord and Tenant Act 1954.

The above represents a summary of the changes to the law affecting leaseholders as a result of the introduction of the Commonhold and Leasehold Reform Act 2002.

Useful addresses

Leasehold Advisory Service (LEASE)
Maple House
149 Tottenham Court Road
London W1T 7BN

Tel: 020 7383 9800

http://www.lease-advice.org

Leasehold Advisory Group (LAG)
Michael Tims and Co
80 Duke Street
Mayfair
London
W1K 6JG

Leasehold Valuation Tribunals
Residential Property Tribunal Service (RPTS)
National Helpline:
Tel: 0845 600 3178
Website: www.justice.gov.uk

Wales1st Floor, West Wing,
Southgate House, Wood Street,
Cardiff CF10 1EW
Tel: 029 2092 2777 Fax: 029 2023 6146
Email: rpt@wales.gsi.gov.uk
Website: http://wales.gov.uk

Other useful addresses
Her Majesty's Stationery Office (HMSO)
Copies of all legislation
regulations and other official publications can be downloaded

from www.legislation.gov.uk.
Alternatively printed copies can be purchased from:
The Stationery Office Ltd (TSO),
PO Box 29, Norwich, NR3 1GN)
Tel: 0870 600 5522
Online ordering: www.tsoshop.co.uk

Association of Residential Managing Agents (ARMA)
178 Battersea Park Road, SW11 4ND
Tel: 020 7978 2607 Fax: 0207 498 6153
Email: info@arma.org.uk
Website: www.arma.org.uk

Association of Retirement Housing Managers (ARHM)
Southbank House,
Black Prince Road, London SE1 7SJ
Tel: 020 7463 0660 Fax: 020 7463 0661
Email: enquirers@arhm.org Website: www.arhm.org

The Royal Institution of Chartered Surveyors (RICS)
12 Great George Street,
Parliament Square,
London SW1P 3AD
Tel: 0870 333 1600
Email: contactrics@rics.org
Website: www.rics.org

The Federation of Private Residents' Associations
PO Box 10271,
Epping CM16 9DB
Tel: 0871 200 3324
Email: info@fpra.org.uk Website: www.fpra.org.uk